Easy Excel for Windows 95

Elaine Marmel

que®

Easy Excel for Windows 95

Copyright © 1995 by Que® Corporation.

Library of Congress Catalog Card Number: 95-71038

International Standard Book Number: 1-56529-0131-6

98 97 96 95   8 7 6 5 4 3 2 1

Interpretation of the printing code: the rightmost double-digit number is the year of the book's first printing; the rightmost single-digit number is the number of the book's printing. For example, a printing code of 95-1 shows that this copy of the book was printed during the first printing of the book in 1995.

Screen reproductions in this book were created by means of the program Collage Plus from Inner Media, Inc., Hollis, NH.

Credits

Publisher
Roland Elgey

Vice President and Publisher
Marie Butler-Knight

Publishing Manager
Barry Pruett

Editorial Services Director
Elizabeth Keaffaber

Managing Editor
Michael Cunningham

Acquisitions Editor
Debbie Abshier

Product Development Specialist
Ella Davis

Production Editor
Kelly Oliver

Copy Editor
Paige Widder

Technical Editors
Richard Eisenmenger
Ed Hanley

Technical Specialist
Cari Skaggs

Book Designers
Barbara Kordesh
Amy Peppler-Adams

Cover Designers
Dan Armstrong
Kim Scott

Production Team
Angela D. Bannan
Claudia Bell
Amy Cornwell
Anne Dickerson
Damon Jordan
Kaylene Riemen
Bobbi Satterfield
Michael Thomas
Scott Tullis

Indexer
Carol Sheehan

Composed in *Stone Serif* and *MCPdigital* by Que Corporation

About the Author

Elaine Marmel is President of Marmel Enterprises, Inc., an organization that specializes in assisting small- to medium-sized businesses computerize their accounting systems.

Elaine spends most of her time writing and is the author of *Word for Windows 2 QuickStart* (also translated into Portuguese and Thai), *Quicken 1.0 for Windows Quick Reference, Quicken 6 for DOS Quick Reference, Using Quicken 2.0 for Windows, The PC User's Mac/The Mac User's PC, Word for Windows 6 Solutions, Word for the Mac Solutions*, and *1-2-3 Release 4 for Windows Solutions*. In addition, Elaine is a contributing editor to *Inside Timeslips* and *Inside Peachtree for Windows*, monthly magazines published about Timeslips 5 and Peachtree for Windows.

Elaine left her native Chicago for the warmer climes of Florida (by way of Cincinnati, OH; Jerusalem, Israel; Ithaca, NY; and Washington, D.C.) where she basks in the sun with her PC and her cats, Tonto and Cato. Elaine also enjoys cross-stitching, and she sings in the Toast of Tampa, the current International Champion Sweet Adeline barbershop chorus.

Trademark Acknowledgments

Contents

Introduction   **2**

Part I: The Basics   **6**

Part II: Entering and Editing Data   **32**

Part III: Making Math Easier   76

Part IV: Managing Files   108

Part V: Formatting the Worksheet   126

Introduction

Microsoft Excel is one of the world's most popular spreadsheet software programs. You could create worksheets on ledger paper and use a calculator, or draw charts on graph paper, but Excel makes these tasks and others related to managing numeric information easier. You can use the program to create worksheets, databases, and charts. You can also automate a lot of your work using macros.

Without a doubt, you could perform the following functions manually, but you can use Excel to make them easier:

- *Lay out a worksheet.* When you sit down to develop a worksheet with a pencil and ledger paper, you don't always have all the information to complete the design and layout of the worksheet. Ideas may occur to you after you sketch the layout of your worksheet. After you're finished jotting down the column headings and the row headings, you might think of another column or row you didn't include. With Excel, you can insert columns and rows easily and move information from one location to another.

- *Calculate numbers.* If you have a checkbook register, you subtract the amount of each check written and add the deposits to the running balance. If you're like me, when you receive your bank statement and balance your checkbook, you find that you made math errors in your checkbook.

  In your checkbook register, you must recalculate the numbers and jot down the new answers. In Excel, you use *formulas*, and you enter them once. Then, when you change the numbers in the worksheet, Excel uses the formulas to recalculate the information in your worksheet and instantly gives you the new answers.

- *Make editing changes.* To correct a mistake on ledger paper, you have to use an eraser, or you have to reconstruct the entire worksheet. With Excel, you can overwrite data in any cell in your worksheet. You can also delete data quickly—in one cell or a group of cells.

- *Undo mistakes.* When you accidentally make mistakes while using Excel, you don't have to retype or reconstruct information. Instead, you can just restore the data with the Undo feature.

■ *Check spelling.* Using Excel's AutoCorrect feature, Excel will correct commonly made mistakes—and you can add your own personal set of "common typos" to the list. In addition, before you print, you can run a spell check to search for misspellings. If you are a poor typist, this feature enables you to concentrate on calculating your numbers and leaves catching spelling errors for Excel.

■ *View data.* When working with a large worksheet, such as a financial statement, you might have to use a ruler to compare figures on a far portion of the worksheet on ledger paper. In Excel, you can split the worksheet into two panes to view distant figures side by side. That way, you can easily see the effects of playing "what if?" scenarios to project changes, and then make the necessary adjustments.

■ *Make formatting changes.* Excel easily enables you to align data in cells; center column headings across columns; adjust column width; display numbers with dollar signs, commas, and decimal points; and other formatting options. You can experiment with the settings until the worksheet appears the way that you want it; then you can print it.

■ *Change how data appears when you print.* You can boldface, italicize, and underline data. Excel also lets you shade cells and add borders. You can also use a different typeface, depending on your printer.

■ *Preview your print job.* You can preview your worksheet to see how it will look when you print it. If you want to make changes before you print, you also can do this in print preview.

■ *Sort data.* You can sort data on the worksheet alphabetically and numerically in ascending or descending order. For example, you can sort a customer invoice report in chronological order by dates. You can also use the AutoFilter feature to quickly find the top or bottom ten values in the list without sorting.

■ *Chart numeric data.* You can track the sales trends of several products with an embedded column chart. Make as many "what if?" projections as you want in the worksheet by increasing and decreasing the numbers. As you change the numbers in the worksheet, Excel instantly updates the embedded chart. Excel's embedded charts let you view simultaneously the sales trends in a picture representation on-screen and the numbers in the worksheet, making your sales forecasting more efficient.

■ *Produce maps.* Using columns of data in your worksheet, you can produce maps that help you perform regional analyses. And, Excel includes some demographic data that you can include in your worksheet to enhance graphic presentations.

■ *Organize lists.* You can create a database to organize your data in a list, such as inventory, employee lists, customer lists, sales records, and so on. In Excel, you can add, delete, sort, search, and display records in the list as often as required to maintain the list.

Task Sections

The task sections include numbered steps that tell you how to accomplish certain tasks, such as saving a workbook or filling a range. The numbered steps walk you through a specific example so that you can learn the task by actually doing it.

Big Screen

At the beginning of each task is a large screen shot that shows how the computer screen will look after you complete the procedure that follows in that task. Sometimes the screen shot shows a feature discussed in that task, however, such as a shortcut menu.

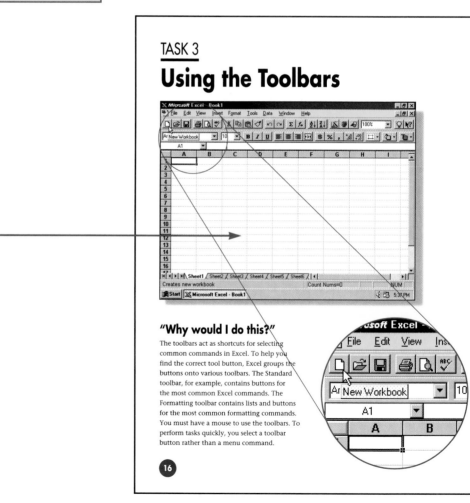

TASK 3

Using the Toolbars

"Why would I do this?"

The toolbars act as shortcuts for selecting common commands in Excel. To help you find the correct tool button, Excel groups the buttons onto various toolbars. The Standard toolbar, for example, contains buttons for the most common Excel commands. The Formatting toolbar contains lists and buttons for the most common formatting commands. You must have a mouse to use the toolbars. To perform tasks quickly, you select a toolbar button rather than a menu command.

16

Step-by-Step Screens

Each task includes a screen shot for each step of a procedure. The screen shot shows how the computer screen looks at each step in the process.

Task 3: Using the Toolbars

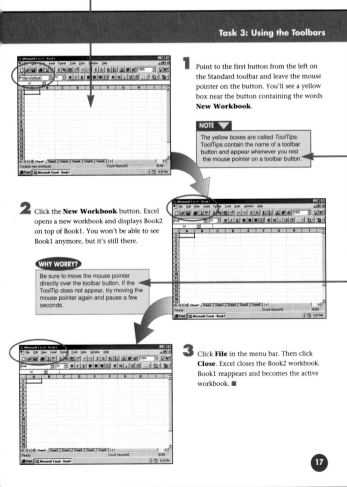

1 Point to the first button from the left on the Standard toolbar and leave the mouse pointer on the button. You'll see a yellow box near the button containing the words **New Workbook**.

NOTE
The yellow boxes are called *ToolTips*. ToolTips contain the name of a toolbar button and appear whenever you rest the mouse pointer on a toolbar button.

2 Click the **New Workbook** button. Excel opens a new workbook and displays Book2 on top of Book1. You won't be able to see Book1 anymore, but it's still there.

WHY WORRY?
Be sure to move the mouse pointer directly over the toolbar button. If the ToolTip does not appear, try moving the mouse pointer again and pause a few seconds.

3 Click **File** in the menu bar. Then click **Close**. Excel closes the Book2 workbook. Book1 reappears and becomes the active workbook. ■

17

Other Notes

Many tasks include other short notes that tell you a little more about certain procedures. These notes define terms, explain other options, refer you to other sections when applicable, and so on.

Why Worry? Notes

You may find that you performed a task, such as sorting data, that you didn't want to do after all. The Why Worry? notes tell you how to undo certain procedures or get out of a situation, such as displaying a Help screen.

PART I
The Basics

Part I of this book introduces you to Excel basics. You need to know some fundamental things about Excel before you start creating your own worksheets. In this part, you will learn how to start and exit Excel. You should ensure that Excel is installed on your hard disk so that, when you click the Start button and view the Programs menu, you see either Microsoft Excel or a folder you know contains Excel. For installation instructions, refer to your Microsoft Excel for Windows 95 documentation. You start and exit Excel as you would any Windows 95 application.

When you start the program, Excel displays a blank *workbook*. The workbook is a file in which you store your data, similar to a three-ring binder. Within a workbook, you have *sheets*, such as worksheets, chart sheets, and macro sheets. A new workbook contains 16 sheets, named Sheet 1 through Sheet 16. You can have up to 255 sheets per workbook, depending on your computer's available memory. Multiple sheets help you organize, manage, and consolidate your data.

A *worksheet* is a grid of columns and rows. The rectangle that appears at the intersection of any column and row is called a *cell*. Each cell in a worksheet has a unique *cell address*. A cell address is the designation formed by combining the row and column names. For example, the cell at the intersection of column A and row 8 is called A8—that's its cell address.

The cell pointer is a cross-shaped pointer (it looks very similar to a Red Cross symbol) that appears over cells in the worksheet. You use the cell pointer to select any cell in the worksheet. The selected cell has a dark border around it and is called the *active cell*. You always have at least one cell selected at all times.

A range is a group of cells. While a range can be a single cell, usually, we use the term *range* when we want to refer to a group of cells. A range can be a column or row of cells, or it can be any rectangular set of cells. When discussing a range, I will refer to the range using a combination of two cell addresses. The first cell address in the range is the address of the uppermost left cell in the range; the second cell address is the address of the lowermost right cell. A colon (:) separates these two elements. For example, the range A1:C3 includes the cells A1, A2, A3, B1, B2, B3, C1, C2, and C3.

The worksheet is much larger than one screen can possibly display at one time. To place data in the many cells that make up the worksheet, you must be able to move to the desired locations. There are many ways to move around the worksheet. You can use the arrow keys to move one cell at a time. You can also use key combinations to quickly move around the worksheet. As you move the cell pointer to a cell, that cell becomes the active cell.

You can navigate around the worksheet with the following arrow keys and key combinations:

To move	Press
Right one cell	→
Left one cell	←
Up one cell	↑
Down one cell	↓
To the beginning of a row	Home
To the end of a row	End+→
To the first cell (A1)	Ctrl+Home
To the last cell (containing data)	Ctrl+End

In Part I, you will learn how to use the shortcut menus. When you point to a single cell or a selected range of cells and then click the right mouse button, Excel displays a *shortcut menu*. This menu appears next to the cell or selected range of cells. The commands on the shortcut menus vary, depending on the cells or object you select in the worksheet.

You also learn how to use the toolbars. Excel has many different *toolbars* that include the tools you use for formatting a worksheet, creating a chart or a map, drawing graphics on the worksheet, creating macros, and many other Excel operations.

This part also discusses some of the ways you can get help in Excel. You can get instant online Help, look at the step-by-step examples, sample files, view the screen tips, and ask the Answer Wizard.

There is one new convention you should note in Windows 95. You do a lot less double-clicking. When you see the instruction *click* in this book, click once using the left mouse button unless directed otherwise.

Starting and Exiting Excel

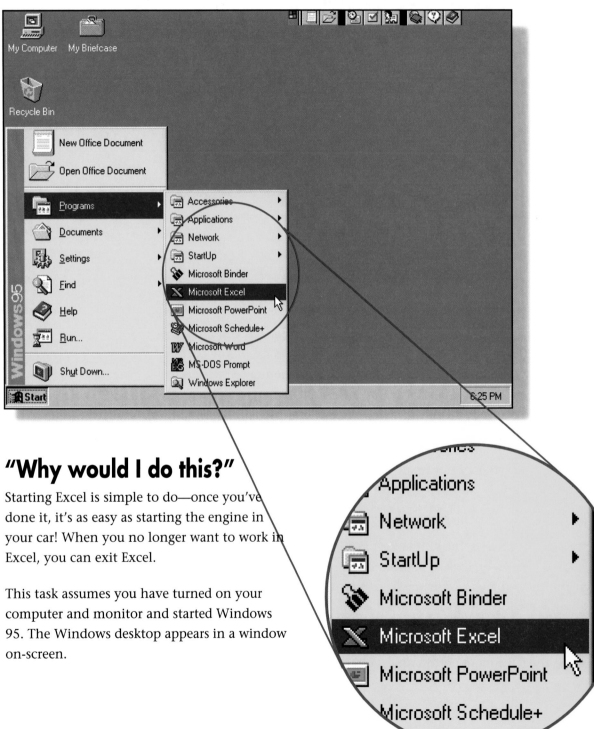

"Why would I do this?"

Starting Excel is simple to do—once you've done it, it's as easy as starting the engine in your car! When you no longer want to work in Excel, you can exit Excel.

This task assumes you have turned on your computer and monitor and started Windows 95. The Windows desktop appears in a window on-screen.

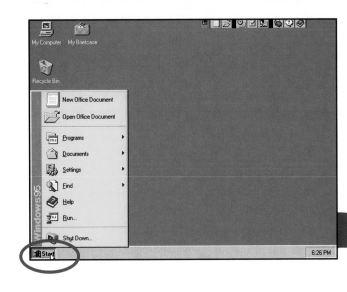

1 Click the **Start** button to display the Start menu.

2 Slide the mouse onto the **Programs** menu. Windows displays the Programs menu choices, which will be different on each computer.

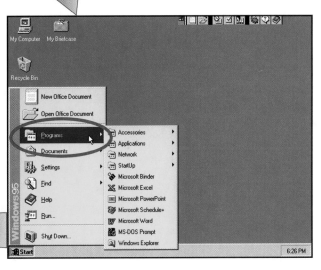

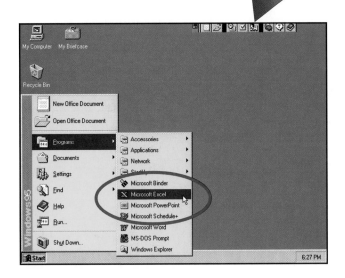

3 Find the **Excel** icon in the list that appears on the Programs menu. If you don't see Excel on the Programs menu, you'll find an icon for Excel in a folder on the Programs menu. Highlight each folder and review its contents.

11

4 Click the **Excel** icon once with the left mouse button. Excel starts, and a blank workbook appears in a window on-screen.

WHY WORRY?

When you're using the mouse to start a program, make sure you click the left mouse button. If nothing happens, check the location of the mouse pointer and make sure you're pointing somewhere on the title for the program before you try clicking again.

5 Click **File** in the menu bar. Then, click **Exit** to close the program and return to the Windows desktop. ■

NOTE ▼

To quickly exit Excel, click the **Close** (**X**) box in the upper right corner of the screen. You may notice two sets of three boxes in the upper right corner. Click the uppermost Close box.

WHY WORRY?

When you first open Excel, you may see an extra toolbar for performing tasks in a networked environment—it's called the WorkGroup toobar. To remove it, click the **View** menu and select the **Toolbars** command. In the Toolbars dialog box, click the **WorkGroup** check box, and then click **OK**.

TASK 2
Using Shortcut Menus

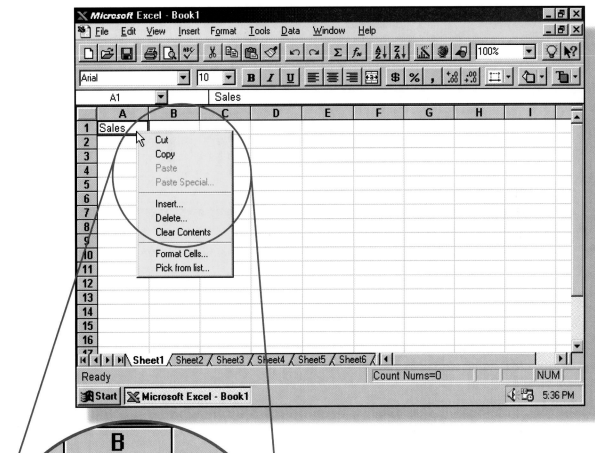

"Why would I do this?"

Excel's shortcut menus include just those commands you need to use for the currently selected cell(s) or an object such as a chart. You might want to use a shortcut menu to quickly edit or format cells. Let's take a look at a shortcut menu that contains editing and formatting commands.

1 Start Excel (as explained in the previous task). When the blank workbook appears, the active cell will be cell A1.

2 Type **Sales** and press **Enter**. This step enters the word **Sales** into cell A1 and makes cell A2 the active cell.

3 Click cell **A1**. This step selects cell A1, making A1 the active cell again—the cell for which you want to open the shortcut menu.

Point inside cell A1 and click the right mouse button. This step opens a shortcut menu. Excel displays a list of editing and formatting commands.

5 Click **Clear Contents** to erase the contents of cell A1. The shortcut menu disappears. ■

WHY WORRY?

Occasionally, you may display a shortcut menu that doesn't have the command you want to use. To leave a shortcut menu without making a selection, press the **Esc** key or click the left mouse button outside the shortcut menu. If you click in a different cell, that cell becomes the active cell.

15

TASK 3
Using the Toolbars

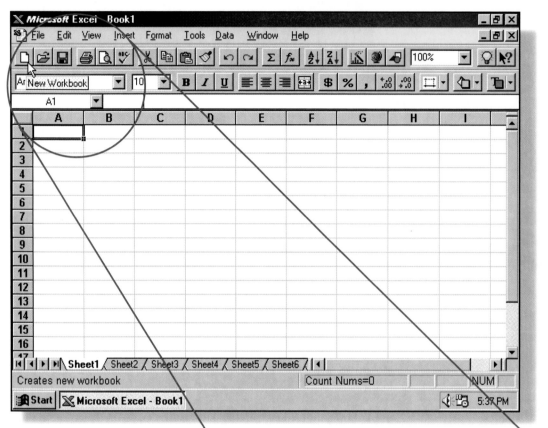

"Why would I do this?"

The toolbars act as shortcuts for selecting common commands in Excel. To help you find the correct tool button, Excel groups the buttons onto various toolbars. The Standard toolbar, for example, contains buttons for the most common Excel commands. The Formatting toolbar contains lists and buttons for the most common formatting commands. You must have a mouse to use the toolbars. To perform tasks quickly, you select a toolbar button rather than a menu command.

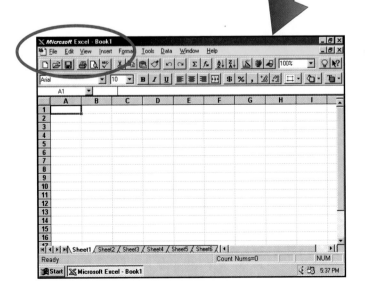

1 Point to the first button from the left on the Standard toolbar and leave the mouse pointer on the button. You'll see a yellow box near the button containing the words **New Workbook**.

2 Click the **New Workbook** button. Excel opens a new workbook and displays Book2 on top of Book1. You won't be able to see Book1 anymore, but it's still there.

3 Click **File** in the menu bar. Then click **Close**. Excel closes the Book2 workbook. Book1 reappears and becomes the active workbook. ∎

Getting Help on Tasks

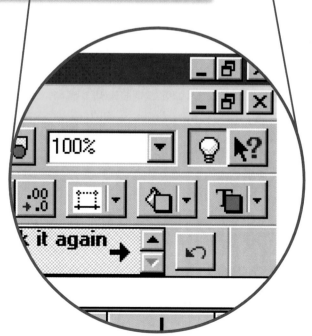

"Why would I do this?"

Excel offers many ways to get help. Excel's TipWizard is an intuitive feature that lets you know when there is a quicker or better way to perform the action that you just performed.

First, let's get some help on how to enter text in cells. Next, we will enter data and then undo the entry. Finally, we will use the TipWizard to get a tip for undoing the entry. Before you start, notice that the TipWizard button, which is the light bulb at the right side of the Standard toolbar, is white.

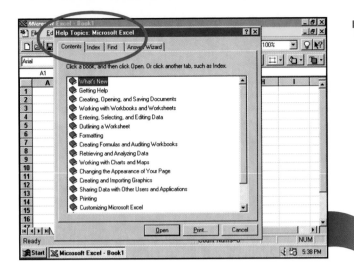

1 Click **Help** in the menu bar. Then click **Microsoft Excel Help Topics**. Excel opens the Help window and displays the Contents tab, which contains a list of help categories. The name of the Help window appears in the title bar.

NOTE ▼

An icon that looks like a book appears to the left of each Help category for which additional information is available.

2 Point to the category **Entering, Selecting, and Editing Data** and double-click the left mouse button. You'll see additional categories available (ones with book icons to their left) as well as Help topics, which have a question mark icon to their left.

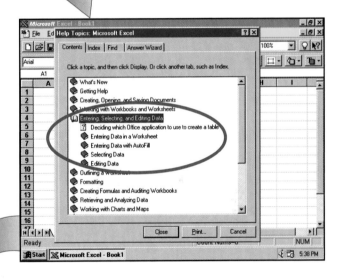

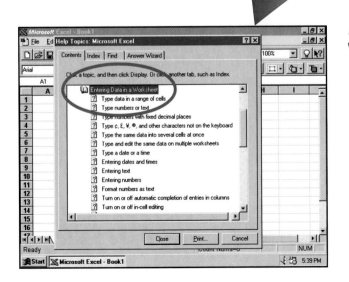

3 Point to the category **Entering Data in a Worksheet** and double-click the left mouse button. You'll see the topics available for this category.

4 Point to the topic **Type Numbers or Text** and double-click the left mouse button. You'll see a window that contains basic information on entering text or numbers and related topics.

WHY WORRY?

To shut the Excel Help window quickly, click the **Close** (**X**) box in the upper right corner of the screen.

5 Click the button that appears next to the topic to jump to it.

NOTE ▼

When the mouse pointer is on a topic for which you can get help, the pointer changes to a hand with a pointing finger.

6 Click cell **A1** to make the worksheet active. You'll see the Help icon in the taskbar.

NOTE ▼

If you know you are finished using Help, make sure Help is the active window and press **Alt+F4**. Or you can minimize Help by clicking the Minimize button in the title bar of the Help window.

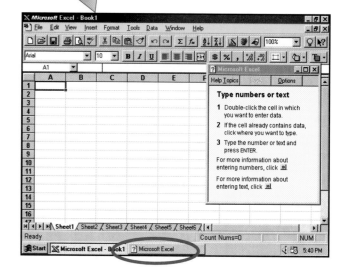

7 Type **sunny** and press **Enter**. As you type, you'll see **sunny** both in cell A1 and in the Formula bar (just below the Formatting toolbar). After you press Enter, the cell pointer moves down to cell A2.

8 Open the **Edit** menu, and then click **Undo Entry**. **Sunny** disappears from cell A1. Notice that the TipWizard button, which is the light bulb near the right end of the Standard toolbar, appears in bright yellow.

NOTE ▼

The TipWizard button lights up after you perform an action, only if Excel has a tip for the action you just performed. If the TipWizard button appears white, Excel has no tip for the action you just performed.

9 Click the **TipWizard** button. Excel displays the TipWizard toolbar. A tip on how to Undo quickly and more efficiently appears in the TipWizard. ■

NOTE ▼

With the TipWizard toolbar displayed, you can click the up- and down-arrow buttons on the TipWizard toolbar to scroll through the list of tips that have appeared during the current session.

21

Getting Help on Menu Commands and Dialog Boxes

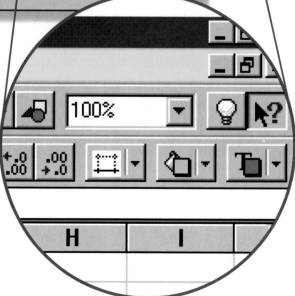

"Why would I do this?"

While you work, you may stumble upon a command on a menu you don't recognize. You don't really want to interrupt your work, but you'd like to know what that command does. Similarly, you may see options in dialog boxes and wonder what those options do—but again, you don't want to interrupt your work. So, instead, use Excel's screen tips.

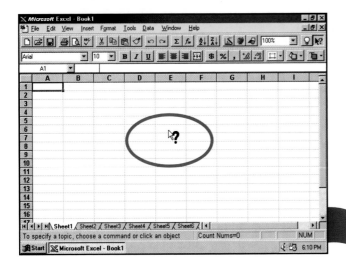

1 When you want help about a menu command, start by clicking the **Help** tool at the right edge of the Standard toolbar. When you move the mouse, you'll notice that the mouse pointer shape changes so that it looks like the icon that appears on the Help tool.

2 Open the **Insert** menu and choose the **Worksheet** command. Instead of executing that command, Excel displays help for it.

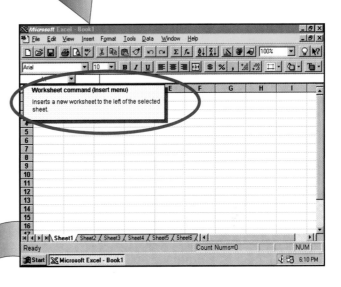

3 To get help on a dialog box option, start by opening that dialog box. For example, open the **Edit** menu and choose the **Go To** command. Excel opens the Go To dialog box. In the Go To dialog box, you see a Special command button.

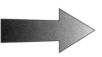

4 Click the **question mark** that appears in the upper right corner of the dialog box. Again, the mouse pointer changes shape to look like the Help tool on the Standard toolbar.

5 Click the item in the dialog box about which you want information. In this example, click the **Special** button. Excel displays a screen tip explaining the item. ■

Moving Around the Worksheet

	A	B	C	D	E	F	G	H
1			Test Scores					
2	**Student**	31-May	30-Apr	31-Mar				
3	Abeles, John	80	68	77				Row: 1
4	Atkinson, Joan	65	66	80				
5	Autry, Spence	73	88	91				
6	Barclay, Joe	95	84	88				
7	Berardinelli, Tom	77	85	66				
8	Burke, George	80	65	88				
9	Chapman, Marla	91	98	84				
10	Chinlund, Robert	68	87	85				
11	Clemens, Ron	66	74	65				
12	Daigle, Marti	88	78	98				
13	Dyer, Tom	84	88	87				
14	Early, Bill	85	77	74				
15	Edberg, Susan	65	79	78				

"Why would I do this?"

Because you typically use many cells in a worksheet, you need shortcuts for moving around the worksheet. Using a mouse is often the easiest way to move around the worksheet—simply use the vertical or horizontal scroll bar to see other portions of the worksheet.

1 Click in cell **A1** and then click four times on the down scroll arrow at the bottom of the vertical scroll bar. Clicking the down scroll arrow moves the worksheet down one row at a time. Notice that row 5 appears at the top of the worksheet.

NOTE ▼

You can point to the up, down, left, or right scroll bar arrow and hold down the mouse button to scroll the worksheet continuously in a particular direction.

2 Click three times on the up scroll arrow at the top of the vertical scroll bar. Clicking the up scroll arrow scrolls the worksheet up one row at a time. Notice that row 2 appears at the top of the worksheet and row 16 (with part of row 17) appears at the bottom of the worksheet.

NOTE ▼

Keep in mind that whatever scroll bar action you perform on a vertical scroll bar can also be performed on the horizontal scroll bar.

3 Click immediately below the solid gray scroll box in the vertical scroll bar itself. Clicking in the shaded area of the scroll bar moves the worksheet up or down one screen at a time. Notice that row 17 appears at the top of the worksheet and the solid gray scroll box is at the bottom of the vertical scroll bar.

4 Drag the scroll box up to the top of the vertical scroll bar. Dragging the scroll box moves the worksheet quickly to a new location in the direction of the scroll box. In this case, Excel moves the worksheet up to the top of the screen and displays the beginning of the worksheet.

NOTE ▼

As you drag, a scroll tip appears in the scroll bar, letting you know the cell that will appear at the top of the screen when you release the mouse button.

5 Move the mouse pointer to the tab split box, the vertical bar located to the left of the horizontal scroll arrow. The mouse pointer changes to a vertical bar with a left and a right arrow.

WHY WORRY?

You can double-click the tab split box to restore the sheet tabs, and you can horizontally scroll to their original display.

6 Drag the tab split box to the left until the box is aligned with the right edge of the Sheet3 tab. Dragging the tab split box to the left displays fewer sheet tabs. In this case, you see the Sheet1, Sheet2, and Sheet3 tabs. Similarly, by dragging to the right, you can display more sheet tabs. ■

TASK 7

Moving to a Specific Cell

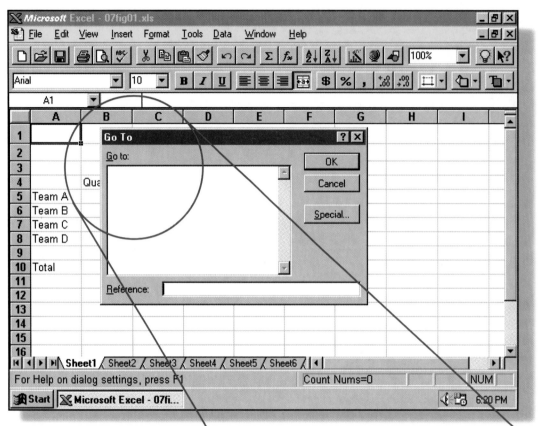

"Why would I do this?"

The Go To command is useful for jumping to cells that are out of view. You can also use the Go To command to select a range of cells. A range of cells is referred to by its first and last cells, separated by a colon. For example, the range B5:E8 includes all the cells between B5, the upper left cell, and E8, the lower right cell. This range starts with cell B5, continues across columns C, D, and E, continues down rows 6, 7, and 8, and ends at cell E8.

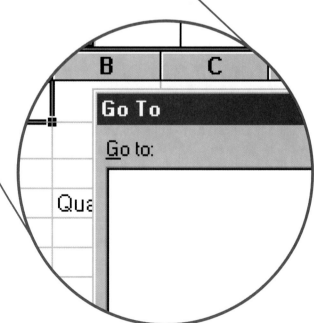

1 Press **F5**. Excel opens the Go To dialog box. The insertion point appears in the Reference text box.

WHY WORRY?

You can easily move between worksheets in a workbook. Click directly on the tab of the worksheet or use the tab scrolling buttons. The Previous and Next Tab buttons (second and third buttons) scroll one sheet at a time. The First and Last Tab buttons (first and fourth buttons) move directly to the first and last sheets.

2 Type **M55**. M55 is the cell to which you want to move the cell pointer. Remember that you refer to cells by their column letter and row number.

3 Press **Enter** or click **OK**. Excel moves the cell pointer to M55, which becomes the active cell. ■

WHY WORRY?

If you mistakenly moved to the wrong cell reference, repeat the Go To command to move to the correct cell. If you selected the wrong range, click any cell to deselect the range.

TASK 8

Selecting Cells

"Why would I do this?"

Knowing how to select a cell is essential because most of the commands and options in Excel operate on the selected cell. You can also select a *range*—a group of adjacent cells. You can even select several ranges at one time with the mouse. For example, there are times when you may want to perform a command on a group of cells that are not adjacent. Maybe you want to change the alignment of text in the top row of the worksheet and a column along the side. To make the change to both ranges simultaneously, you need to select both ranges at the same time.

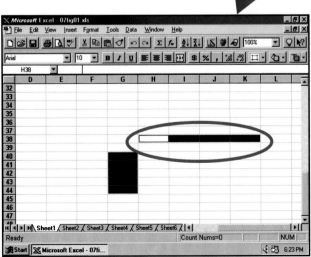

1 Click cell **G40** to make it the active cell. Notice the cell pointer outlines the selected cell.

NOTE ▼
If, as your next action, you click cell F40, you also deselect cell G40.

WHY WORRY?
If you select the wrong cell or range, click the correct cell.

2 Hold down the mouse button and drag the mouse down the column through cells **G40**, **G41**, **G42**, **G43**, and **G44**. Then release the mouse button. You just selected the range **G40:G44**.

NOTE ▼
Remember, a range is indicated by the address of the upper left cell, a colon (:), and the address of the lower right cell.

3 Hold down the **Ctrl** key and select **H38**; then drag the mouse to select cells **I38**, **J38**, and **K38**. Release the mouse button and then release the Ctrl key. Notice the first range **G40:G44** remains selected, and the second range **H38:K38** is also selected. ■

PART II

Entering and Editing Data

You can enter four types of data into an Excel worksheet: text, numbers, calculations, and dates. The good news for you is that you enter and edit each type of entry in a similar fashion. However, to make Excel robust enough to handle your needs, each type of data you enter has its own characteristics.

Text entries are sometimes called *labels*. Excel aligns labels with the left side of a cell. Labels can contain letters, symbols, numbers, or any combination of these characters. Even though a text entry may contain numbers, Excel cannot use it for numeric calculations. An example of a label is a title to describe the type of worksheet you want to create. A title such as 1994 ANNUAL BUDGET gives meaning to the columns and rows of numbers that make up a budget worksheet. *Column headings* are labels that describe what the numbers represent in a column. You can enter column headings to specify time periods such as years, months, days, dates, and so on. Similarly, *row headings* are labels that describe what the numbers represent in a row. You can enter row headings to identify income and expense items in a budget, subject titles, and other categories.

Numeric entries are called *values*. Excel aligns values with the right side of a cell. Values contain numbers and other symbols. Numeric entries must begin with a numeral or one of the following symbols: +–, (. or $. The period is used as a decimal point for decimal values. You might find it quicker to enter numeric data by typing the numbers and using the Enter key on your numeric keypad.

In Excel, calculations are called *formulas*. Excel displays the result of a formula in a cell as a numeric value and aligns it with the right side of a cell. You use numbers in various cells to make calculations. For instance, Excel can recognize the number in a cell, add it to the number in a different cell, and display the result of the formula in another cell.

Dates are recognized by Excel as values and appear aligned with the right side of a cell. Dates in a worksheet can help you keep track of any time-dependent information. For example, you can track the last time you modified your worksheet or the last time you

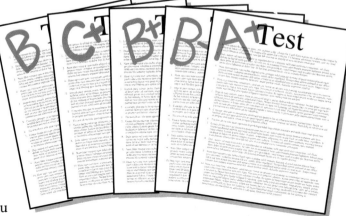

placed a sales call. You can also enter dates in a report to show when items are posted or when transactions are done. You can use dates in formulas to calculate, for example, the next date you want to place a sales call. Excel recognizes an entry as a valid date only if you enter the date in one of the date formats accepted by Excel. The following table shows the Excel date formats you would enter in a cell and sample results:

Format	Example
MM/DD/YY	9/12/94
DD-MMM-YY	12-Sep-94
DD-MMM	12-Sep (assumes the current year)
MMM-YY	Sep-94 (assumes the first day of the month)

Times are treated the same way as dates by Excel and can be used in the same ways you use dates. Time entries are values and appear aligned with the right side of a cell. Entering a time in a worksheet is especially useful for keeping track of the last time you worked on the worksheet. Or, perhaps you want to create a time table or time study. Excel recognizes an entry as a valid time only if you enter the time in one of the time formats accepted by Excel. The following table shows the Excel time formats you would enter in a cell and sample results:

Format	Example
HH:MM	13:45 (24-hour clock)
HH:MM AM/PM	2:45 AM (12-hour clock)
HH:MM:SS	13:45:06 (24-hour clock)
HH:MM:SS AM/PM	2:45:06 PM (12-hour clock)

There are three methods for entering data in an Excel worksheet: 1) type the data and press Enter, 2) type the data and press an arrow key, and 3) type the data and click the check mark in the formula bar. The formula bar is located beneath the Formatting toolbar. When you enter data in a cell, Excel displays an X and a check mark in the formula bar. If you click the X, Excel rejects the entry; if you click the check mark, Excel accepts the entry.

After you enter data, you can undo mistakes, overwrite a cell, edit the information in a cell, erase data, copy information, and move data to other locations in the worksheet. You also can insert and delete cells, rows, and columns, sort and find information, and check spelling in your worksheet.

Entering Text and Numbers

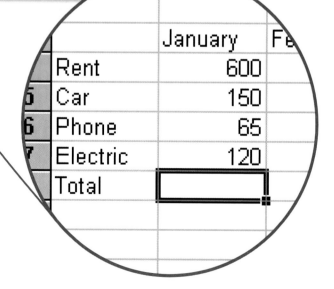

"Why would I do this?"

Most people use worksheets primarily to track or calculate numbers. To give meaning to the columns and rows of numbers that make up a worksheet, you can give them names to describe what the numbers represent. Excel calls these names *labels*. While you can enter information in any order, you will find it most useful to enter labels before you enter numbers. That way, you enter numbers into the appropriate cells.

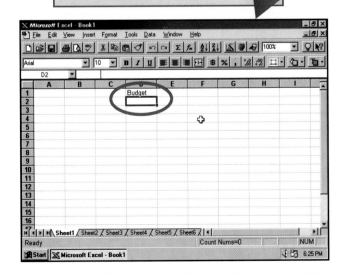

1 Click cell **D1** to make it the active cell. The active cell on a worksheet appears as a white cell with a bold border.

2 To give your worksheet a title, type **Budget**. Notice that, before you press Enter, the entry appears in the formula bar and in cell D1. The mode indicator in the lower left corner of the screen (above the Windows taskbar) displays **Enter**.

> **NOTE** ▼
>
> An X and a check mark appear to the left of the entry in the formula bar. Clicking the X cancels the change; clicking the check mark confirms the new entry and stores the information in the cell.

3 Press **Enter**. Excel accepts the entry and makes D2 the active cell. Notice that the word **Budget** is left-aligned.

> **NOTE** ▼
>
> Excel always moves down one cell when you type data and press Enter.

37

4 Select cell **B3**—we'll use B3 to enter a label for the first column heading.

5 Type **January** and press the right-arrow key. Excel accepts the entry, enters the label into the cell, and makes C3 the active cell.

WHY WORRY?

If you make a mistake when typing an entry, use the Backspace key to correct the entry. Excel does not place the entry in the cell until you press Enter, press an arrow key, or click the check mark in the formula bar.

6 Type **February** and press the right-arrow key. Then, type **March** and press the right-arrow key. Cell E3 is now the active cell.

7 Type **Total** and press **Enter**. Then, starting in cell A4, type the remaining data that appears in the figure next to this step so that your computer screen matches the screen shown here.

8 Click cell **E1** and type **12-Sep**. Click the check mark in the formula bar to accept the entry, enter the date in the cell, and make E1 remain the active cell.

NOTE ▼

In the cell, the date appears as **12-Sep**, but Excel stores the date in a different format. In the formula bar, you see **9/12/1995**. Notice that the date is right-aligned.

9 Click cell **F1** and type **10:00**; then click the check mark in the formula bar. Excel accepts the entry, enters the time in the cell, and makes F1 remain the active cell. ■

NOTE ▼

In the cell, the time appears as **10:00**, but the time is stored in a different format. In the formula bar, you see **10:00:00 AM**. Notice that the time is right-aligned.

39

TASK 10
Using Undo

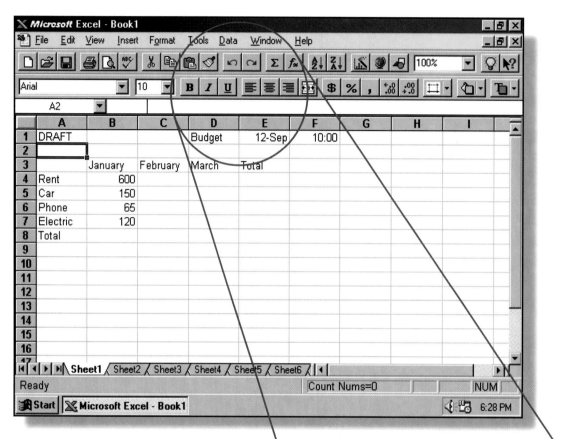

"Why would I do this?"

The Undo feature recovers the most recent changes to worksheet data. For instance, if you edit the worksheet and make a mistake, you can use Undo to reverse the last editing command you performed before you save a worksheet. Undo becomes very helpful when you need to correct editing and formatting mistakes, especially when you delete data that you did not intend to delete.

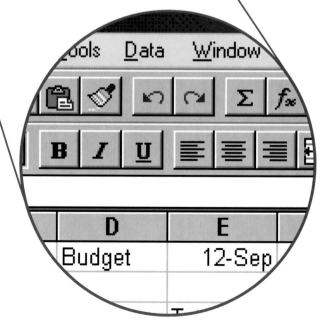

1 To see how the Undo feature works, first enter a label into cell A1. Click cell **A1**, type **DRAFT**, and press **Enter**.

2 Click the **Undo** button on the Standard toolbar. Or, open the **Edit** menu and choose the **Undo** command. Excel removes the entry in cell A1. ■

WHY WORRY?

Click the **Undo** button a second time on the Standard toolbar to "undo" the undo.

Editing a Cell

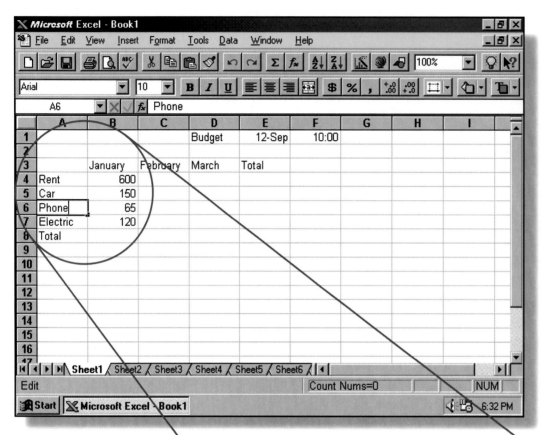

"Why would I do this?"

By editing a cell, you can correct data after it is placed in a cell. You can make changes to part or all of the information in a cell.

Once you know how to edit your data, you can just make a few quick changes to correct the contents of a cell. You'll save a lot of time correcting long entries because you won't have to type an entire entry over again. If the new entry is entirely different, however, then overwriting the entry may turn out to be faster.

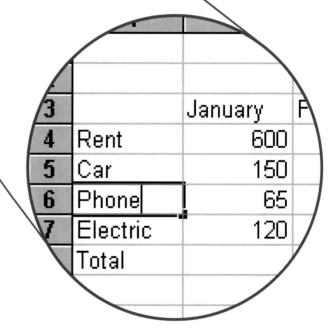

1 Double-click inside cell **A6**—the entry you want to change—to the right of the text that appears in the cell. Double-clicking a cell displays the insertion point in the cell at the location where you double-clicked. In this case, when you click to the right of the text that appears in the cell, the insertion point will appear at the end of the cell entry. You are now in Edit mode. Notice that the X and check mark appear in the formula bar.

2 Press **Home**. The insertion point moves to the beginning of the entry.

NOTE

You can use the arrow keys to move the insertion point to the characters you want to change.

3 Type **Tele** to add these letters to the beginning of the current label, **Phone**. Next, we will change the capital P to a lowercase p.

43

4 Press **Ins**. Pressing the Ins key while you work in Edit mode lets you overwrite characters. When you press Ins, Excel highlights the character immediately to the right of the insertion point—in this case, the letter P. Whenever numbers or characters appear highlighted while you work in Edit mode, typing will replace the highlighted character with the character you type.

5 Type **p**. Excel replaces the highlighted letter, capital P, with a lowercase p and highlights the next letter, h.

WHY WORRY?

If you make a mistake when typing the entry in Edit mode, use the **Delete** key or the **Backspace** key to correct the entry. Excel does not place the entry in the cell until you press Enter or an arrow key.

6 Press **Enter**. Excel accepts the new entry and makes A7 the active cell. ■

NOTE ▼

If the change is minor, you can edit the cell, or you can overwrite the information in the cell by simply typing over it. Overwriting a cell is handy when a cell contains the wrong data. Or, you can erase the cell by selecting the cell and pressing the **Delete** key.

Copying or Moving a Cell

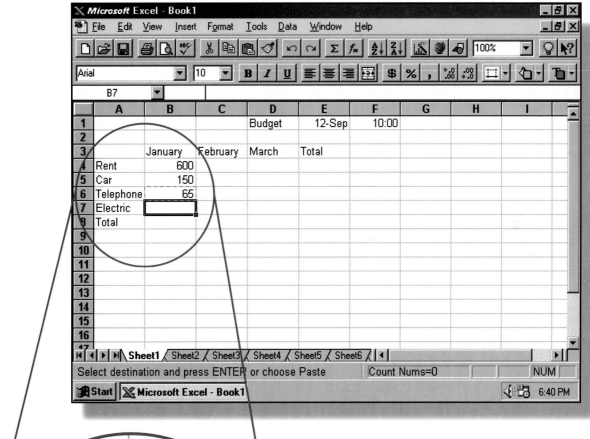

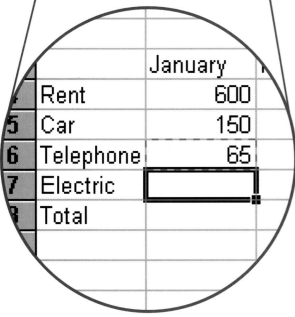

"Why would I do this?"

You can save the time of retyping information on the worksheet by copying or moving a cell. For example, you might want to copy a label from one cell to another cell. That way you won't have to type the label over again, saving you time and keystrokes.

Excel's Move command lets you remove information from one cell and place it into another cell. You do not have to go to the new cell and enter the same data and then erase the data in the old location.

1 Select cell **B6** to make it the active cell. The formula bar displays the current entry—the entry you want to copy.

2 To copy a cell, click the **Copy** button on the Standard toolbar. To move a cell, click the **Cut** button on the Standard toolbar. A dashed "marquee" surrounds the cell you are copying or cutting. The status bar reminds you how to complete the task: **Select destination and press ENTER or choose Paste**.

3 Select cell **B7** so that you can copy or move the information to this cell. Notice that the dashed marquee still appears around B6, the cell you copied or cut.

NOTE ▼

You can press **Ctrl+C** to select the Copy command or **Ctrl+X** to select the Cut command. You can also select the commands from the **Edit** menu.

4 Click the **Paste** button on the Standard toolbar to paste a copy of the data into the cell. As you can see, the entry appears in cell B7. Excel copies the entry and the format (alignment, protection settings, and so on). If you cut instead of copied, the original entry in cell B6 would have disappeared. ■

NOTE ▼

You can press **Ctrl+V** to select the Paste command; you can also select it from the **Edit** menu.

WHY WORRY?

After copying or cutting a cell, the dashed marquee remains so you can use the arrow keys to move to another cell and click the Paste button again. When you finish copying or cutting, remove the marquee by pressing **Esc**.

Moving and Copying Using Drag and Drop

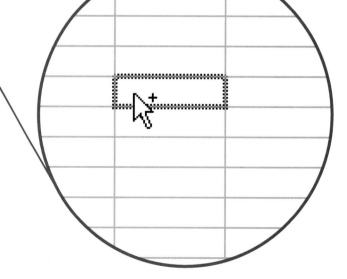

	A	B	C	D	E	F	G	H	I
1				Budget	12-Sep	10:00			
2									
3		January	February	March	Total				
4	Rent	600							
5	Car	150							
6	Telephone	65							
7	Electric	65							
8	Total								

Drag to copy cell contents, use Alt key to switch sheets   Count Nums=1   NUM

"Why would I do this?"

Sometimes, you only need to copy or move information once—from one location to another. Using a technique known as *drag and drop*, you can use the mouse to drag information from one location to another quickly.

1 Click the cell containing the information you want to move or copy; for this example, click **B5**.

2 Place the tip of the mouse pointer on any edge of the cell. The mouse pointer shape changes from a plus sign to an arrow pointing up and to the left.

3 The first part of the copy or move operation involves dragging the information you want to move or copy. To copy information, first press and hold the **Ctrl** key and then press and hold the mouse button. When you press Ctrl, the mouse pointer shape changes slightly—you'll see a small plus sign attached to the arrow.

4 Without releasing the mouse button and the **Ctrl** key, drag the mouse pointer to the new location by sliding the mouse on your desktop. In our example, drag the mouse pointer to **D7**. As you drag, the cell pointer outline appears shaded.

NOTE ▼

If you're moving information, drag the mouse pointer to the new location by sliding the mouse on your desktop.

5 To complete the operation (the "drop" portion of "drag and drop"), release the mouse button and the **Ctrl** key. Excel places the contents of the original cell at the new location. If you copied, Excel also leaves the contents of the original cell at its initial location. If you moved, Excel removes the contents of the original cell. ■

NOTE ▼

If you're moving information, complete the operation by releasing the mouse button.

WHY WORRY?

If you "drop" the cell too soon, use the Undo tool to restore the worksheet to its original appearance and try again.

Filling a Range

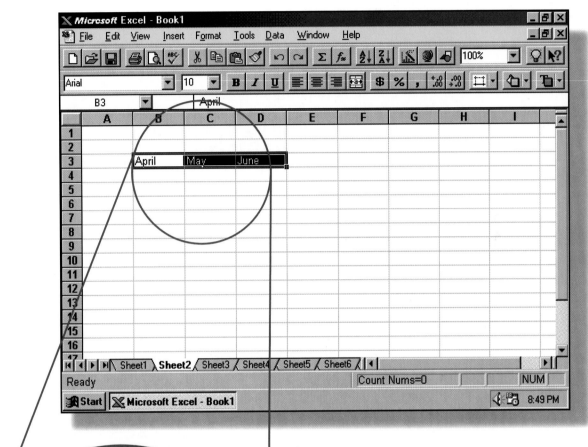

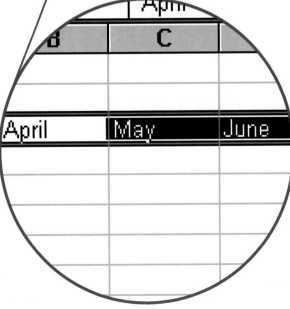

"Why would I do this?"

Much of the activity in setting up a worksheet revolves around filling a range of cells with consecutive values. Perhaps you may need to fill the top row of your budget worksheet with month names. While you could type this information, you can save a lot of time by using Excel's Edit, Fill Series command.

You can also use the Edit, Fill Series command to fill a range with evenly spaced values; for example, you may want the names of alternating months (instead of each month) to appear at the top of your budget worksheet.

1 Click the **Sheet2** tab and then click cell **B3**. Excel selects Sheet2 and moves this sheet to the top, making it the active sheet. We'll use B3 to enter the first column heading.

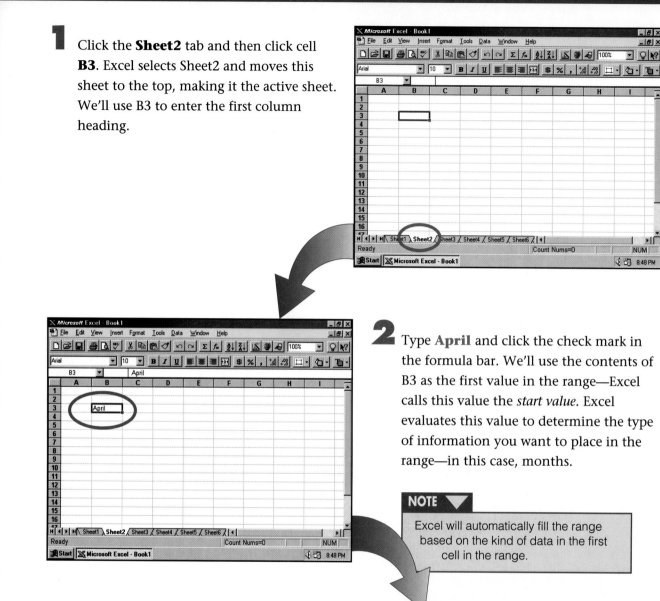

2 Type **April** and click the check mark in the formula bar. We'll use the contents of B3 as the first value in the range—Excel calls this value the *start value*. Excel evaluates this value to determine the type of information you want to place in the range—in this case, months.

NOTE ▼

Excel will automatically fill the range based on the kind of data in the first cell in the range.

3 Move the mouse pointer to the lower right corner of the current cell's border. The mouse pointer changes to a black plus sign.

4 Drag the cell's border to cells **C3** and **D3** and release the mouse button. Excel fills the range with months.

WHY WORRY?

To undo the fill series, click the **Undo** button on the Standard toolbar immediately after filling the range.

5 To fill a range with a series of evenly spaced values, follow the same basic steps. Type the first two values of the series into the first two cells in the range. For example, type **January** in cell A3 and leave the word **April** in cell B3. Don't worry about the contents of cells C3 and D3—we'll overwrite them.

6 Select both cells and move the mouse pointer to the lower right corner of the selection's border. Again, the mouse pointer changes to a black cross.

Drag the selection's border to expand the range you want to fill—**A3:D3**.

Release the mouse button. Excel fills the range. In our example, Excel fills the rest of the selection range with the months July and October. ∎

Inserting and Deleting Rows and Columns

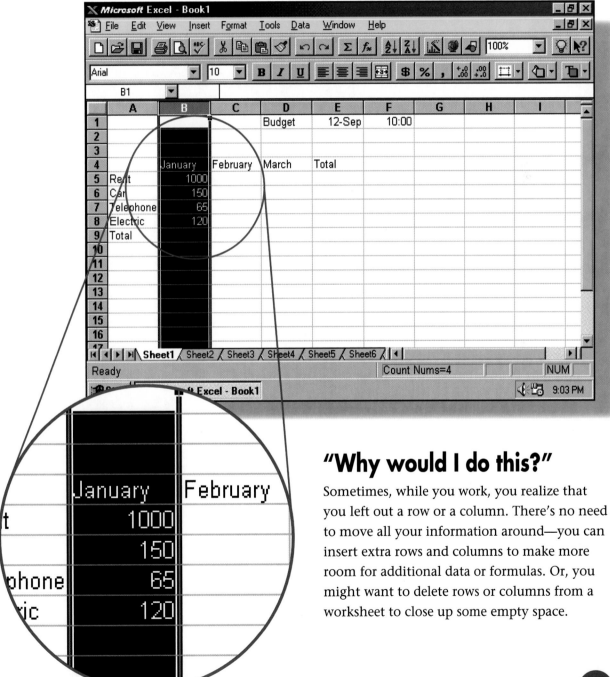

"Why would I do this?"

Sometimes, while you work, you realize that you left out a row or a column. There's no need to move all your information around—you can insert extra rows and columns to make more room for additional data or formulas. Or, you might want to delete rows or columns from a worksheet to close up some empty space.

1 Click the **Sheet1** tab; then click cell **C2**. This moves Sheet1 to the top and selects cell C2. Selecting a cell helps Excel figure out where you want to insert a new row or column. Excel will insert the new row above row 2.

NOTE ▼

Excel inserts new rows *above* the selected cell and new columns to the *left* of the selected column.

2 Click **Insert** in the menu bar and then click **Rows**. Excel inserts a new row above row 2 and moves down all rows below the cell pointer. The same process works for inserting columns.

3 Next, let's delete a column. Click the column letter at the top of column **B**. Be sure to click the column letter, not a cell in the column. When you click the column letter, Excel selects the entire column. (Column B is the column you want to delete.)

NOTE ▼

You can select an entire row by clicking on the row number.

4 Select **Edit** in the menu bar and then select **Delete**. Excel deletes the column, and shifts all columns to the right of column B left one column.

5 Click any cell in the worksheet to deselect the range. ■

NOTE ▼

If you see the Delete dialog box, you did not select the entire column. Click the **Entire Column** button and then click **OK**.

WHY WORRY?

To undo a row insertion/deletion or a column insertion/deletion, click the **Undo** button in the Standard toolbar.

Freezing Column and Row Titles

"Why would I do this?"

Often, you will enter data in a worksheet that exceeds more than one screen, requiring you to scroll to the right or down to view other areas. Use the Freeze Panes command to freeze column and row titles so that they remain on-screen when you scroll to other parts of the worksheet.

1 Click the cell where you want to freeze the titles; for this example, click cell **B5**.

2 Click **Window** in the menu bar and then click **Freeze Panes**. This step splits the window into panes and freezes the titles above and to the left of the cell pointer.

> **NOTE** ▼
>
> A horizontal line splits the window into a top and bottom pane, and a vertical line splits the window into a left and right pane.

3 Repeatedly click the arrow at the right edge of the horizontal scroll bar to display the far right side of the worksheet. As you can see, the row titles that appear in Column A remain on-screen.

59

4 Press **Ctrl+Home**. This step returns the cell pointer to the location it appeared when you chose the Freeze Panes command.

5 Repeatedly click the arrow at the bottom edge of the vertical scroll bar to display the bottom portion of the worksheet. As you can see, the column titles remain on-screen.

6 Click **Window** in the menu bar and then click **Unfreeze Panes**. Excel restores the worksheet to the original display. ∎

WHY WORRY?

If you freeze the panes in the wrong place, simply select the **Window**, **Unfreeze Panes** command and try again.

Hiding and Displaying Columns and Rows

"Why would I do this?"

You can hide columns and rows so they can't be seen or printed. This feature is useful if you create a large worksheet and don't need to see certain portions of it while you work. Or, perhaps you work with sensitive data and you do not want other people to see information on your screen or printout.

1 Select any cell in each column you want to hide. If you want to hide columns B, C, and D, select a cell in each.

WHY WORRY?

When you hide columns or rows, the formulas that use data in the hidden columns will continue to work properly.

NOTE ▼

Excel does not allow you to hide only part of a column.

2 Click **Format** in the menu bar, click **Column**, and then click **Hide**. Excel hides the selected columns. You can tell by the column letters (A, E, F) that columns B, C, and D are hidden.

NOTE ▼

If you move the cell pointer after step 2, you must select a range that includes the hidden columns before you perform step 3.

3 Next, let's redisplay the hidden columns. Click **Format** in the menu bar, click **Column**, and then click **Unheeded**. Excel redisplays the hidden columns. ■

WHY WORRY?

If you hide the wrong columns, click the **Undo** button on the Standard toolbar to display the recently hidden columns.

Sorting Data

"Why would I do this?"

Excel's Sort feature lets you organize text in alphabetical order and numbers in numeric order. The text and numbers can be sorted in ascending (lowest to highest) or descending (highest to lowest) order.

You might want to sort a column of row headings so that you can easily look down the sorted column to find the information you want.

1 Click the **Sheet3** tab. Starting in cell **A1**, type the data that appears in the figure next to this step so your computer screen matches the figure shown here.

NOTE ▼

Keep in mind that you can sort by any column, sort more than one column, and sort in ascending or descending order. For complete information on these options, see your Microsoft Excel documentation.

2 Hold down the mouse button and drag the mouse to select the range **A4:C8**. Be sure to select all the data in the rows; otherwise, the entries will be mismatched. Be sure not to select the column headings.

NOTE ▼

You can also select A4:C8 by selecting cell **A4**, holding down the **Shift** key, and moving the cell pointer to cell **C8**.

3 Click the **Sort Ascending** button on the Standard toolbar. Then click any cell to deselect the range. Excel sorts the data in alphabetical order according to the item names. ■

WHY WORRY?

If the sort does not work as you planned, immediately click the **Undo** tool on the Standard toolbar or select the **Edit**, **Undo Sort** command.

Filtering a List of Information

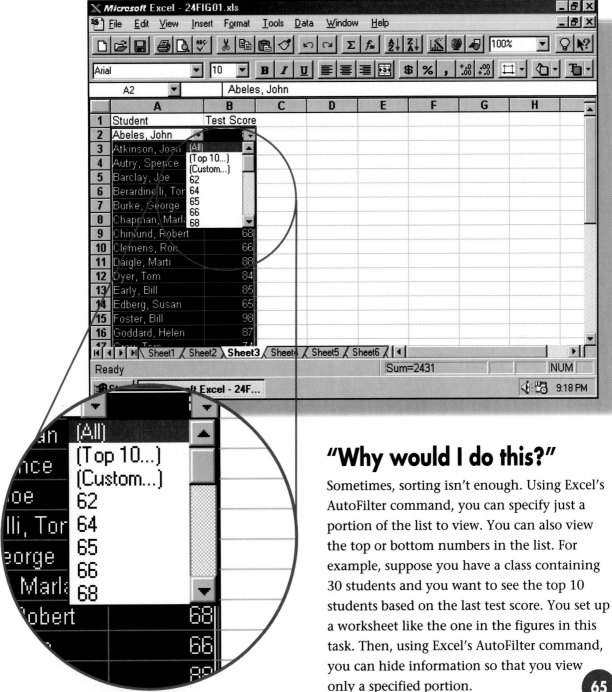

"Why would I do this?"

Sometimes, sorting isn't enough. Using Excel's AutoFilter command, you can specify just a portion of the list to view. You can also view the top or bottom numbers in the list. For example, suppose you have a class containing 30 students and you want to see the top 10 students based on the last test score. You set up a worksheet like the one in the figures in this task. Then, using Excel's AutoFilter command, you can hide information so that you view only a specified portion.

65

1 Set up your worksheet so that it contains all the information you want to store. In the example shown here, the data is stored in cells **A1:B32**.

> **NOTE** ▼
>
> Keep in mind that you can filter by any column and by more than one column. For complete information on these options, see your Microsoft Excel documentation.

2 Hold down the mouse button and drag the mouse to select all the data; in the example, I selected the range **A2:B32**. Be sure to select all the data in the rows; otherwise, the entries will be mismatched. Be sure not to select the column headings.

> **NOTE** ▼
>
> You can also select A2:B32 by selecting cell **A2**, holding down the **Shift** key, and pressing the right-arrow key, the **End** key, and then the down-arrow key.

3 Choose the **Data** menu, **Filter**, and then **AutoFilter**. Excel adds list box buttons to the first entry in each column of the selected data.

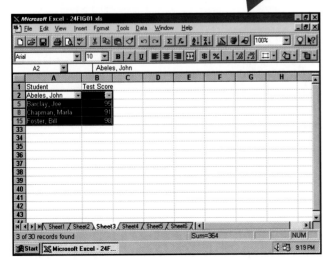

4 Click the list box in the Test Scores column. Excel shows you the choices by which you can filter the list to display only those items you want to see.

NOTE ▼

To remove the list box tabs from the tops of the columns, choose **Data**, **Filter**, **AutoFilter** again.

5 Choose **Top 10**. You see the Top 10 AutoFilter dialog box. From this dialog box, you can choose to view the bottom portion of the list, choose more or less than 10 items to view, or choose to view items in the list or items that fall within a percentage.

In our example, if you choose **Top** and **10** for the first two boxes, choosing **Percent** in the last box would show you the students whose scores fell in the top 10 percent of all the scores.

6 Choose **OK**. Excel displays the list as the items in it meet the criteria you just set. ■

WHY WORRY?

If you don't see the list you expected to see, reopen the list box in the first cell of the Test Scores column and choose **(All)** from the top of that list box. Excel will redisplay the entire list and you can try again.

TASK 20

Finding and Replacing Data

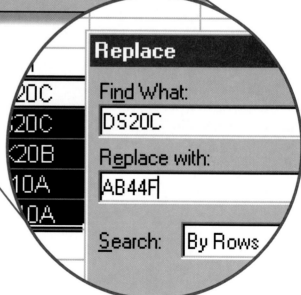

"Why would I do this?"

With Excel's Find and Replace features, you can locate data and then replace the original data with new data.

When you have a label, a value, or formula that is entered incorrectly throughout the worksheet, you can use the Edit, Replace command to search and replace all occurrences of the incorrect information with the correct data.

1 Hold down the mouse button and drag the mouse to select the range you want to search. For this example, select cells **A4** to **A8**.

2 Open the **Edit** menu and choose the **Replace** command. Excel displays the Replace dialog box. The insertion point is in the Find What text box.

3 Type the text you want to find and replace. For this example, type **DS20C**.

4 Click in the **Replace with** text box or press the **Tab** key and type the label you want to use as a replacement. For this example, type **AB44F**.

> **NOTE** ▼
>
> The case you use matters. Excel will replace existing uppercase text with lowercase text if you supply lowercase text in the Replace with text box.

5 Click the **Replace All** button to begin the search. When Excel finishes replacing all occurrences, click outside the range to deselect it. (In this example, Excel replaced all occurrences of **DS20C** with **AB44F**.) ∎

> **NOTE** ▼
>
> Be sure that you want to replace all occurrences before you select the Replace All button. You can also search for and replace one occurrence at a time. Select the list you want to search before you choose the **Edit**, **Replace** command and then use the **Replace** button in the Replace dialog box.

> **WHY WORRY?**
>
> To undo the replacements, click the **Undo** button on the Standard toolbar immediately after replacing the data.

Checking Your Spelling

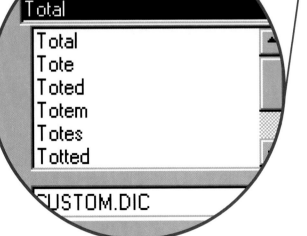

"Why would I do this?"

Excel's spell checker rapidly finds and high-lights for correction the misspellings in a worksheet. Spell checking is an important feature that makes your worksheets look professional and letter-perfect.

1 Click **Sheet1**. If you've been following along with the examples in this book, the worksheet should look like the one shown in the figure next to this step. Go to cell **C4**, and remove the first occurrence of the letter **r** in the word **February**.

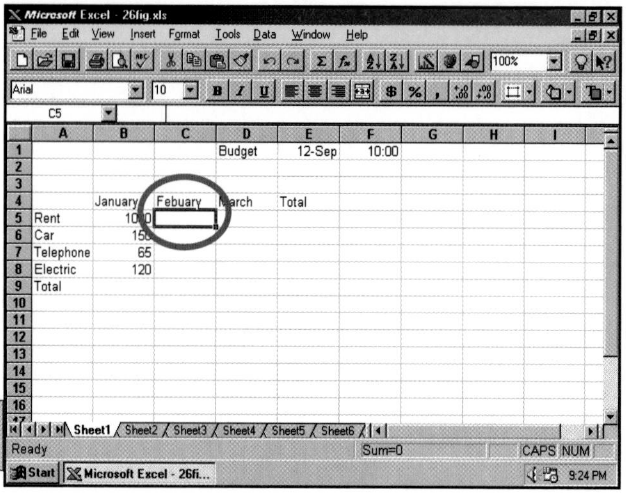

NOTE ▼

Remember, you can double-click a cell to edit it, and then press **Enter** when you're finished.

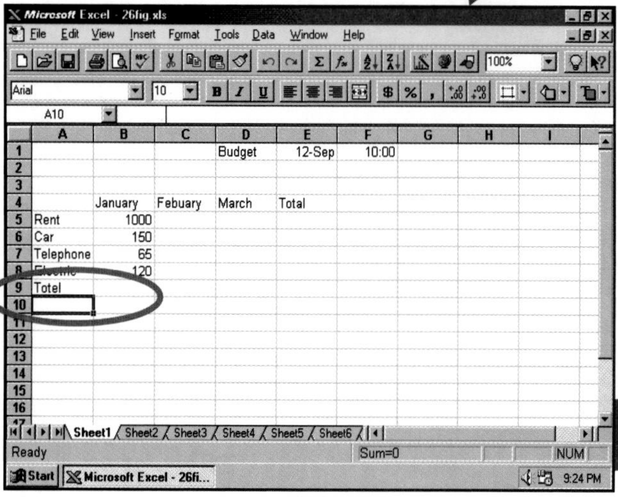

2 In cell **A9**, change the **a** in the word **Total** to an **e**.

3 Select cell **A1**. When you select the first cell in the worksheet, Excel begins spell checking at the top instead of the middle of the worksheet.

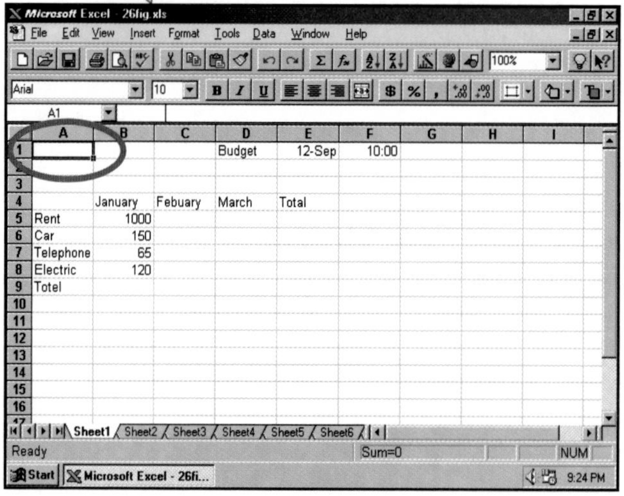

4 To begin the spell checker, click the **Spelling** button on the Standard toolbar (the button with the check mark and ABC text). Excel finds the first misspelled word (**Febuary**) and displays the word at the top of the Spelling dialog box. The correct word (**February**) appears in the Change To box and in the Suggestions list.

NOTE ▼

The Spelling dialog box lists suggested spellings for the word not found in the dictionary.

5 Click **Change**. Excel then replaces the incorrect word with the correct word in the worksheet. The spell checker finds the next misspelled word (**Totel**) and displays it at the top of the Spelling dialog box.

WHY WORRY?

If the first word in the Suggestions list is not the word you need, click the down scroll arrow in the **Suggestions** list to find the correct word. When you see the word, click it. Excel selects the word and displays it in the **Change To** box.

6 Click **Change**. Again, Excel replaces the incorrect word. Then, Excel displays a dialog box that tells you spell checking is completed. Click **OK**. Now you can see the corrected spelling error in **February** in cell C4, and **Total** in cell A9. ■

WHY WORRY?

If you mistakenly select the wrong Spell option, you can click the **Undo Last** button in the Spelling dialog box.

TASK 22

Using AutoCorrect

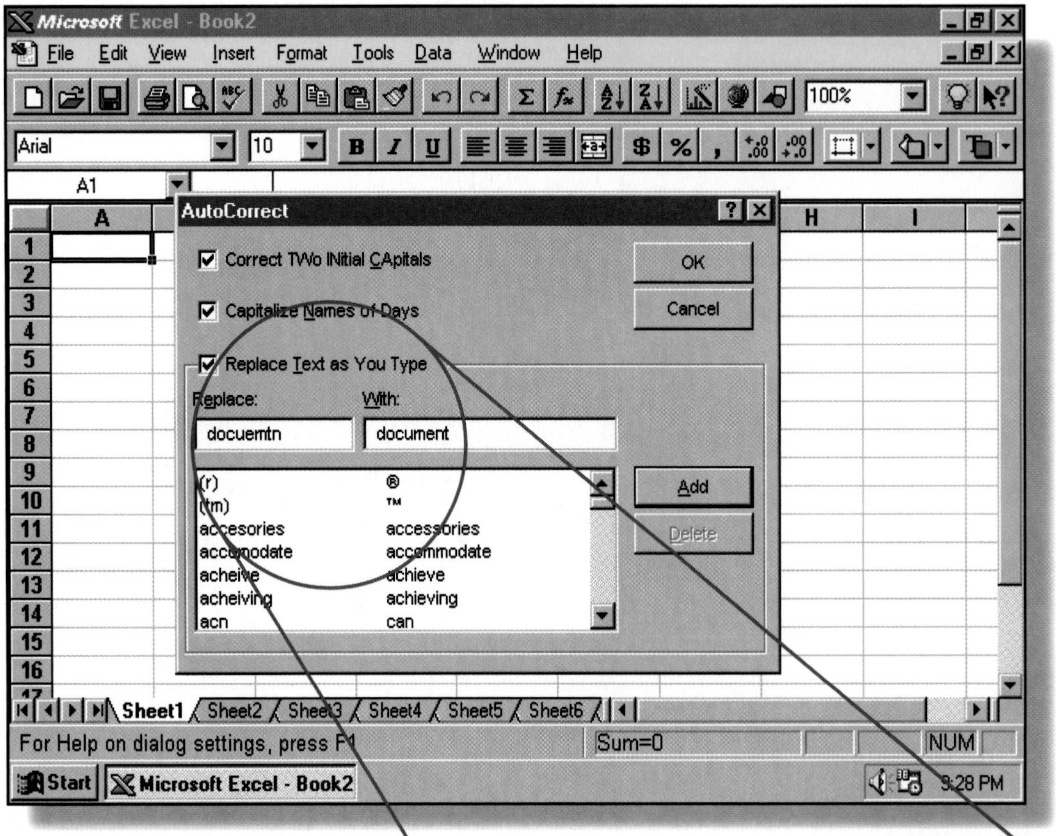
Microsoft Excel - Book2
File Edit View Insert Format Tools Data Window Help
Arial
10
100%
A1
AutoCorrect
Correct TWo INitial CApitals
Capitalize Names of Days
Replace Text as You Type
Replace:
With:
docuemtn
document
(r) ®
(tm) ™
accesories accessories
accomodate accommodate
acheive achieve
acheiving achieving
acn can
OK
Cancel
Add
Delete
Sheet1 Sheet2 Sheet3 Sheet4 Sheet5 Sheet6
For Help on dialog settings, press F1
Sum=0
NUM
Start
Microsoft Excel - Book2
3:28 PM

"Why would I do this?"

All of us have certain words we misspell consistently. How about "teh" for "the"? Using the AutoCorrect feature in Excel, you can define a list of your own personal most commonly mistyped words, and Excel will automatically correct them when you mistype them.

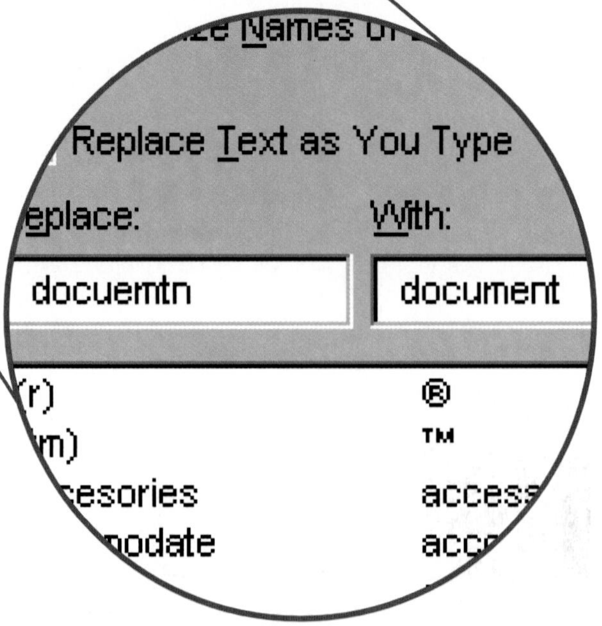
Replace Text as You Type
With:
docuemtn
document
®
™

1 Choose the **Tools** menu; then select **AutoCorrect**. Excel displays the AutoCorrect dialog box. By default, Excel will change two uppercase letters that appear one right after another to upper-case and lowercase. Excel will also capitalize days of the week. If you don't want Excel to make these changes, remove the checks from the check boxes by clicking the check boxes.

2 The third check box in this dialog box indicates that Excel will make the corrections that appear in the list below while you type. To add a typographical error to the list, type the wrong spelling in the **Replace** text box. Then, type the correct spelling in the **With** box.

WHY WORRY?

If you no longer want Excel to make a particular correction, reopen the Auto-Correct dialog box, highlight that correction in the list, and click **Delete**.

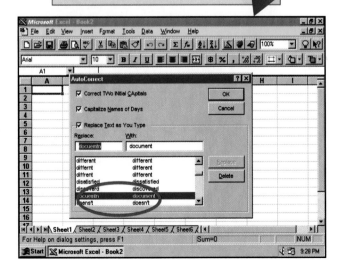

3 Press **Enter** to place your typographical error in the list. Choose **OK** when you finish entering mistakes and want to close the AutoCorrect dialog box. ■

NOTE ▼

Whenever you type one of the words that appears in the Replace box of the AutoCorrect dialog box, Excel will automatically change that word to the version you supplied in the With box.

PART III
Making Math Easier

Now that you know how to enter data and change your worksheet data using various editing techniques, it's time to learn about using worksheets to make math easier. In Excel, you use *formulas* to add, subtract, multiply, and divide numbers and *functions* to total cells and calculate averages. In Part III, you'll learn about one of the most powerful features available in a worksheet—copying a formula so that you don't need to re-enter it. To make things even easier, you'll also learn how to assign an English name to a range of cells.

Formulas use cell references to calculate the values in other cells of the worksheet. Once you enter a formula, you can change the values in the referenced cells, and Excel automatically recalculates the formula's value based on the cell changes. You can include any cells in your formula. The cells do not have to be next to each other. Also, you can combine mathematical operations—for example, C3+C4–D5.

Functions are abbreviated formulas that perform a specific operation on a group of values. Excel provides over 250 functions that can help you with tasks ranging from determining loan payments to calculating the natural logarithm of a number.

The SUM function is particularly useful when you need to add a column of numbers, since the SUM function is a shortcut for entering a formula that automatically sums entries in a range. The format for entering any function is basically the same—you start with an equal sign (=) to tell Excel you're entering a function. Then you type the function name and enclose any arguments in parentheses. The SUM function consists of the function name—SUM—and the range of cells you want to add; you enter the range within parentheses. To enter a SUM function, first you type **=SUM(**. You can type the function in lowercase or uppercase letters. The open parenthesis tells Excel you are going to specify *arguments* for the function. Arguments are parameters (such as a range containing values) that Excel needs to make the calculation. In the case of the SUM function, you'll specify a range to add by selecting the range. A dashed border called a *marquee* surrounds the selected range. Finally, you type a close parenthesis. Typing **)** tells Excel that you are finished specifying arguments. For the SUM function, Excel inserts the range coordinates in the parentheses.

The AVERAGE function is a predefined formula that calculates the average of a list of numbers just the way you learned to do in high school—the AVERAGE

$$E=mc^2$$

function adds the values you specify in a range and then divides the sum by the number of values in the range. You can use the Function Wizard button (the one with **fx** on it) in either the formula bar or in the Standard toolbar to help you enter the AVERAGE function instead of typing the function. In fact, the Function Wizard button can help you create any function, and it is particularly helpful when you are unsure of the correct syntax for the function.

$$f(x)$$

For information on creating complex formulas, the order of precedence (the order in which Excel evaluates formulas), and functions, refer to your Microsoft Excel documentation.

In Excel, there are three types of cell references: relative, absolute, and mixed. The type of cell reference you use in a formula determines how Excel changes the formula when you copy it into a different cell. The formulas you create in this section contain *relative cell references*. This means that when you copy a formula from one cell to another, the cell references in the formula change to reflect the cells at the new location of the formula. That means that you can create a formula in Column A that adds numbers in Column A, and then copy that formula to Column B, and Excel will adjust the formula to add numbers in Column B.

When you use an *absolute cell reference* in a formula, you force Excel to use the same cell reference when you copy the formula. There are certain formulas you might want to create in which you want an entry to always refer to one specific cell value. For example, when showing sales by region, you might want to calculate each region's percentage of total sales. The total sales amount (and cell address) remains unchanged, or absolute. So, in the formula that calculates each region's percentage of total sales, you use an absolute cell reference when you refer to the cell containing total sales. When you copy this formula, the total sales cell reference always refers to the one cell that contains the total sales for all regions.

A *mixed cell reference* in a formula contains both a relative and an absolute cell reference. A mixed cell reference is helpful when you need a formula that always refers to the values in a specific column, but the values in the rows must change, and vice versa.

TASK 23

Adding and Subtracting Data with a Formula

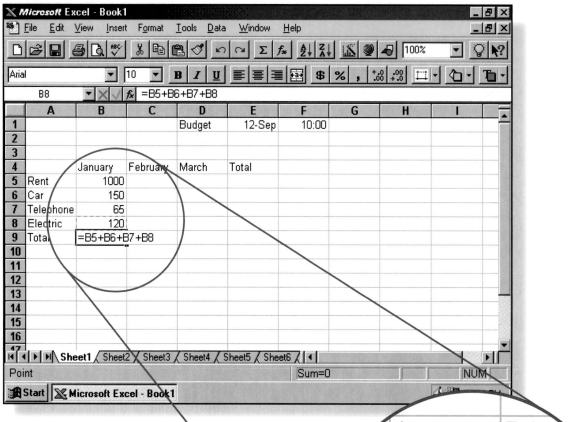

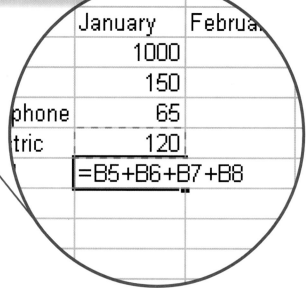

"Why would I do this?"

Because a formula references cells rather than values, Excel updates the sum whenever you change the values in cells. In an expense report, you might want to enter a formula to sum your expenses. Similarly, you could just subtract the values in the cells, but if you change any of the values, the result is not current. To learn how to enter a subtraction formula, we'll create a balance sheet on Sheet4.

1 Click cell **B9**. In this cell, we'll place a formula, and Excel will display the result of the formula. Type = (an equal sign).

> **NOTE** ▼
>
> Typing = tells Excel that you want to create a formula. You then select the cells you want to include in this formula.

2 Click cell **B5**; it is the first cell you want to include in the addition formula. Excel surrounds the cell with a dashed marquee. You see **=B5** in the formula bar and in cell B9.

> **WHY WORRY?**
>
> If you make a mistake typing, use the **Backspace** or **Delete** keys to correct the mistake. If you click the wrong cell, just click the correct cell.

3 Type +. The plus sign (+) is the *operator*. It tells Excel which mathematical operation you want to perform—in this case, addition. You see **=B5+** in the formula bar and in cell B9. The cell pointer returns to B9.

81

4 Click cell **B6**; it is the second cell you want to include in the addition formula. A dashed marquee surrounds the cell. You see **=B5+B6** in the formula bar and in cell B9.

5 Repeat Steps 3 and 4 until you have also included B7 and B8 in your formula. Cell B8 is the last cell you want to include in the addition formula. You see **=B5+B6+B7+B8** in the formula bar and in cell B9. Your worksheet should look like the one in the figure next to this step.

6 Press **Enter** to tell Excel that you are finished creating the formula. You see the result of the formula (**1335**) in cell B9. Whenever B9 is the active cell, the formula **=B5+B6+B7+B8** appears in the formula bar.

7 Now let's try subtracting. Click the **Sheet4** tab to move to Sheet4. Starting in cell A1, type the data that appears in the figure next to this step so that your computer screen matches the figure shown here.

WHY WORRY?

If, immediately after entering the addition formula, you discover the formula is wrong, delete it by clicking the **Undo** button on the Standard toolbar.

8 Click cell **B6**, where we will place the formula. Excel will display the result of the formula. Type =.

9 Select cell **B3**; it is the first cell you want to include in the subtraction formula. Excel surrounds the cell with a dashed marquee. You see **=B3** in the formula bar and in cell B6.

10 Type –. The minus sign (–) is the operator. It tells Excel which mathematical operation you want to perform—in this case, subtraction. You see **=B3–** in the formula bar and in cell B6. The cell pointer returns to B6.

11 Select cell **B4**; it is the second cell you want to include in the subtraction formula. A dashed box surrounds the cell. You see **=B3–B4** in the formula bar and in cell B6.

WHY WORRY?

If you select the wrong cell, click the **Undo** button on the Standard toolbar.

12 Press **Enter** to tell Excel that you are finished creating the formula. You see the result of the formula (**38000**) in cell B6. Whenever B6 is the active cell, the formula **=B3–B4** appears in the formula bar. ■

NOTE ▼

If you see number signs (#) in the column, the entry is too long. You must change the column width (see Part V).

Multiplying and Dividing Data with a Formula

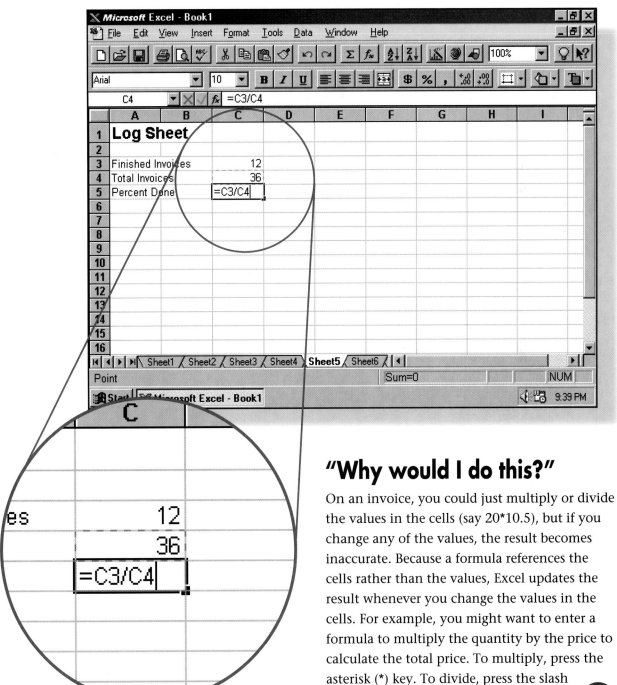

"Why would I do this?"

On an invoice, you could just multiply or divide the values in the cells (say 20*10.5), but if you change any of the values, the result becomes inaccurate. Because a formula references the cells rather than the values, Excel updates the result whenever you change the values in the cells. For example, you might want to enter a formula to multiply the quantity by the price to calculate the total price. To multiply, press the asterisk (*) key. To divide, press the slash (/) key.

1 Click the **Sheet5** tab to move to Sheet5. Starting in cell A1, type the data that appears in the figure next to this step so that your computer screen matches the figure shown here.

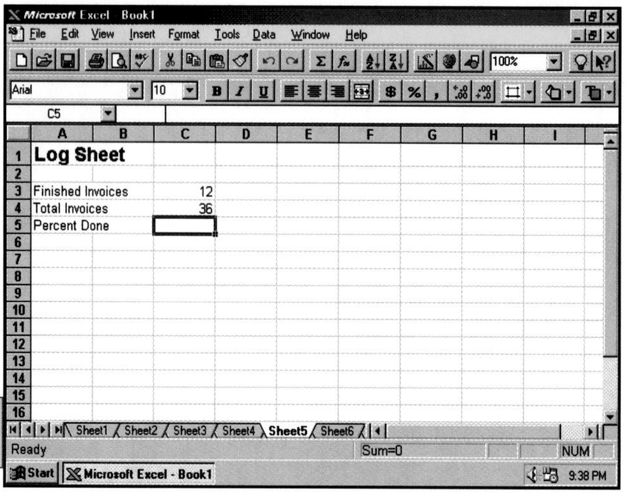

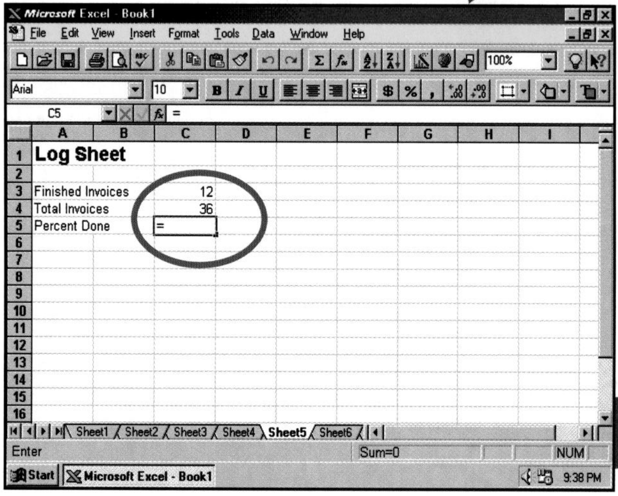

2 Click cell **C5**, where we will place the formula. Excel will display the result of the formula. Type =.

> **NOTE** ▼
>
> Typing an equal sign (=) tells Excel you want to create a formula. You then select the cells you want to include in the formula.

3 Select cell **C3**; it is the first cell you want to include in the formula. A dashed marquee surrounds the cell. You see **=C3** in the formula bar and in cell C5.

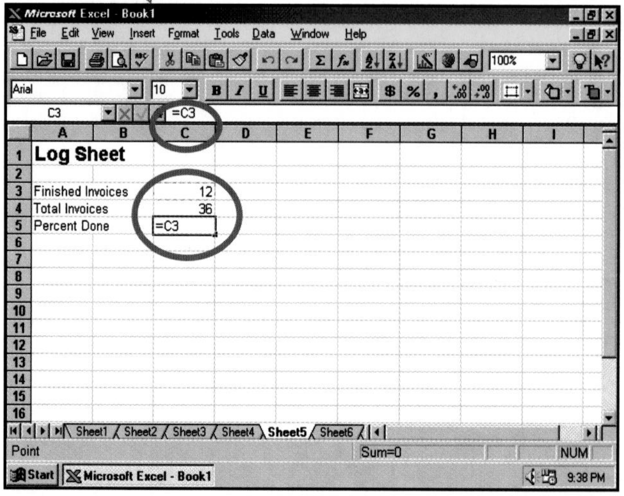

4 Type /. The slash (/) is the operator. It tells Excel which mathematical operation you want to perform—in this case, division. The cell pointer returns to C5.

5 Select cell **C4**. Including cell C4 tells Excel to divide Finished Invoices by Total Invoices. A dashed marquee surrounds the cell. You see **=C3/C4** in the formula bar and in cell C5.

WHY WORRY?

If you make a mistake while entering the division formula, immediately click the **Undo** button in the Standard toolbar to delete the most recent entry.

6 Press **Enter**. You see the result of the formula (**0.333333**) in cell C5. Whenever C5 is the active cell, **=C3/C4** appears in the formula bar. ■

NOTE ▼

If you see number signs (#) in the column, the entry is too large to fit in the column. You must change the column width (see Part V).

87

Totaling Cells with the SUM Function

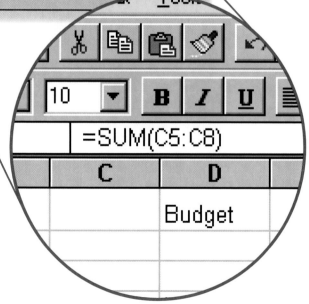

Microsoft Excel - Book1.xls

File Edit View Insert Format Tools Data Window Help

Arial		10		B	I	U						$	%	,						

C9 =SUM(C5:C8)

	A	B	C	D	E	F	G	H	I
1	**Budget**			Budget	12-Sep	10:00			
2									
3									
4		January	February	March	Total				
5	Rent	1000	1000	1000					
6	Car	150	150	150					
7	Telephone	65	65	65					
8	Electric	120	120	120					
9	Total	1335	1335						
10									
11									
12									
13									
14									
15									
16									

Sheet1 / Sheet2 / Sheet3 / Sheet4 / Sheet5 / Sheet6 /

Ready — Sum=1335 — NUM

Start | Microsoft Excel - Boo...

=SUM(C5:C8)

"Why would I do this?"

A function is a predefined formula. You provide the variable parts of the formula, and Excel calculates the result. Using the SUM function, you can add the numbers that appear in a range of cells. If you later insert or delete rows (or columns), Excel automatically updates the total.

Because adding long rows of numbers is such a common activity, Excel includes the AutoSum button on the Standard toolbar to make entering the function easier.

1 Click the **Sheet1** tab to move to the budget on Sheet1. Then, select the range **B5:B8** by selecting cell B5 and dragging the mouse down to cell B8. B5:B8 is the range that contains the numbers you will use to fill columns C and D.

2 Move the mouse pointer to the fill handle in the lower right corner of cell B8 until the mouse pointer changes to a cross. Then drag the selected range across columns C and D. This step fills the range C5:D8 with the numbers from column B.

3 Click cell **C9**, where you will place the SUM function.

4 Double-click the **AutoSum** button on the Standard toolbar to enter the SUM function in the formula bar and in the cell. **=SUM(C5:C8)** appears in the formula bar. You see the result of the formula, **1335**, in cell C9.

NOTE ▼

If you single-click the AutoSum button, you'll see the formula in cell C9 before Excel places its result in the cell. Clicking a second time accepts the formula, and you see the result of the formula in C9.

5 Repeat the basics of steps 3 and 4 to enter the SUM function in cell E5. Click in cell **E5** and double-click the **AutoSum** button. **=SUM(B5:D5)** appears in the formula bar. You see the result of the formula, **3000**, in cell E5. ■

WHY WORRY?

If you prefer using the keyboard, you can press **Alt+=** to create a SUM formula. Then, press **Enter** to place the formula in the active cell.

WHY WORRY?

To delete the most recent entry, click the **Undo** button in the Standard toolbar immediately after entering the SUM function.

Calculating an Average

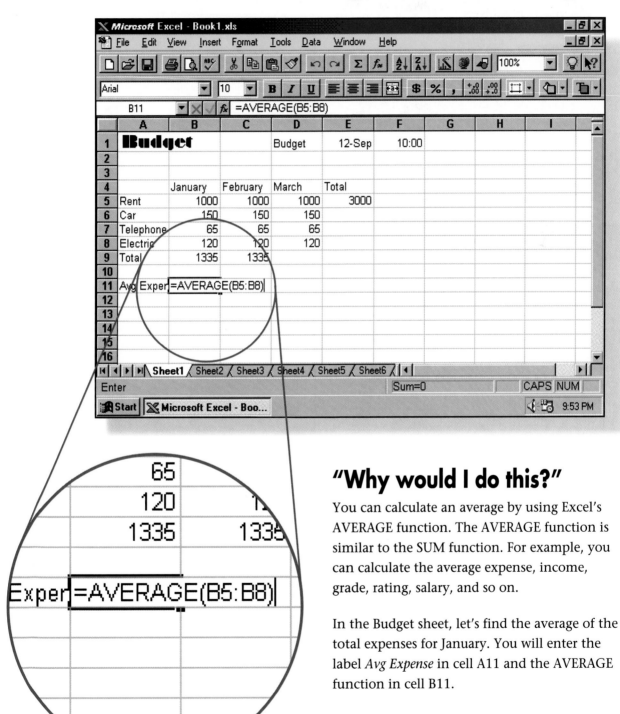

"Why would I do this?"

You can calculate an average by using Excel's AVERAGE function. The AVERAGE function is similar to the SUM function. For example, you can calculate the average expense, income, grade, rating, salary, and so on.

In the Budget sheet, let's find the average of the total expenses for January. You will enter the label *Avg Expense* in cell A11 and the AVERAGE function in cell B11.

1 In **Sheet1**, click cell **A11**, type **Avg Expense**, and press the right-arrow key. B11 is the cell in which you want to place the formula that calculates an average.

> **NOTE** ▼
>
> Notice that the long label spills into cell B11. You can widen column A to accommodate the long entry. See Part V.

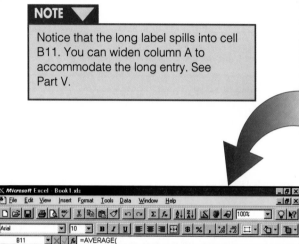

2 Type **=AVERAGE(**. AVERAGE is the name of the function that automatically averages entries in a range. You enter the range that you want to average within the parentheses. (You can type the function in lowercase or uppercase letters.)

3 Hold down the mouse button and drag the mouse to select cells **B5**, **B6**, **B7**, and **B8**. This step selects the range B5:B8. In the formula bar and in cell B11, you see **=AVERAGE(B5:B8**. A marquee surrounds the selected range.

4 Type **)** to tell Excel that you are finished selecting the range. Excel inserts the range in the parentheses. In the formula bar and in cell B11 you see **=AVERAGE(B5:B8)**.

5 Press **Enter** to confirm the formula. You see the result of the function, **333.75**, in cell B11. ■

WHY WORRY?

To delete the most recent entry, click the **Undo** button in the Standard toolbar immediately after entering the AVERAGE function.

Using AutoCalculate

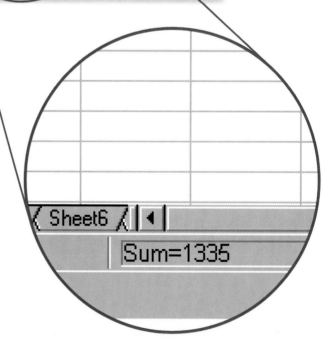

"Why would I do this?"

Many times, while you're working in a worksheet, you want to know the sum of a group of numbers but you don't need to save that sum. That means that you want to create a SUM function, but you don't really want to include it in the worksheet. Using the AutoCalculate feature of Excel, you can get a quick sum, average, or count of values without actually entering a function into a cell.

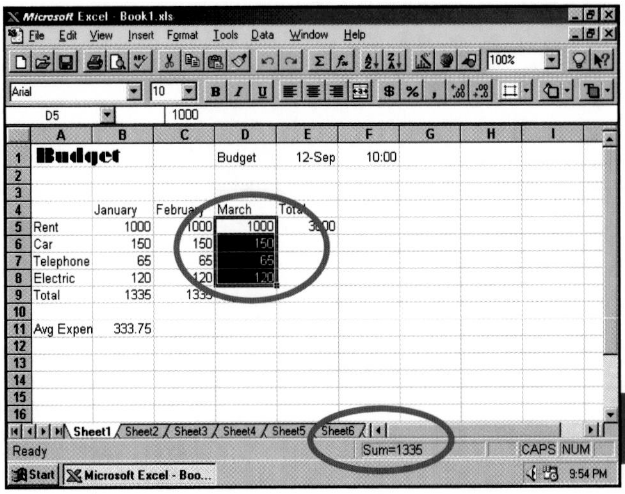

1 In the **Budget** worksheet, select cells **D5:D8**. Look at the lower right portion of the status bar, where you'll see that Excel has added the selected range and displayed the result.

2 To see the average or count of the selected range, move the mouse pointer into the status bar and click the right mouse button. Select the appropriate choice.

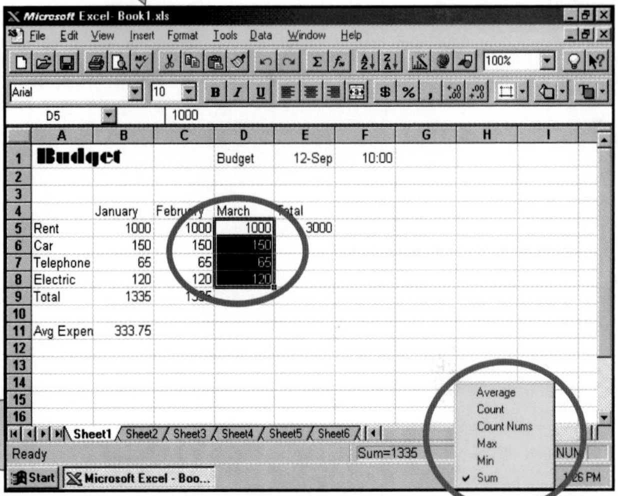

> **NOTE** ▼
>
> Use the COUNT function in Excel to count the number of cells that contain numeric values in a specified range. For example, this function is useful when you want to count the number of students in the class that you listed in your worksheet.

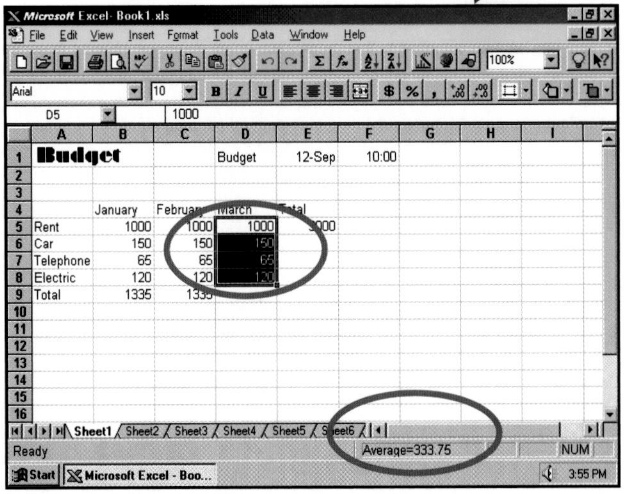

3 In the figure next to this step, I selected **Average**. Notice that the average appears in the status bar where the sum used to appear. ■

Using the Function Wizard

"Why would I do this?"

What do you do when you want to try a function but you don't know how to set it up? Suppose you want to save money for a special birthday present. You deposit $50 into a savings account that earns 6 percent annual interest compounded monthly (monthly interest of 6 percent/12, or 0.5 percent). You plan to deposit $5 at the beginning of every month for the next 12 months. How much money will be in the account at the end of 12 months? Use Excel's future value function and let the Function Wizard help you set up the function.

1 Click the **Sheet6** tab to display Sheet 6. Place the cell pointer in cell **A1** and click the **Function Wizard** button on the Standard toolbar.

2 In the Function Wizard dialog box, click **Financial** in the Function Category list on the left. Then click **FV** in the Function Name list on the right.

NOTE ▼

The structure of the function and its arguments appear immediately below the Function Category list. The structure for the present value function in Excel is **FV(rate,nper,pmt,pv,type)**.

3 Click the **Next** command button. Excel displays the second Function Wizard dialog box, where you are prompted to enter values for each argument of the function.

NOTE ▼

If you want to move between text boxes using the keyboard, press the **Tab** key. Pressing the **Enter** key is the same as clicking the Finish button.

97

4 For the *rate*, Excel indicates that you should enter the rate per period. That means that 6 percent annually is .5 percent monthly, and you would enter the decimal equivalent of .5 percent, **.005**.

> **NOTE**
>
> You can enter **.5%** or even the formula **6%/12** and Excel will convert the value to .005.

5 The *nper* represents the total number of payments you intend to make while you save. Since you will deposit money monthly for one year, you enter **12**.

6 For *pmt*, supply the amount of money you intend to deposit each month. In our example, you would type **–5**.

> **NOTE**
>
> For the FV and PV functions, all money that you put out, such as payments and initial deposits, should be represented as negative values. Think of them as "outflows" from your pocket.

7 *Pv* is optional and represents the amount of money you initially deposit. In our example, you would type **–50**.

8 Use the **Type** box to tell Excel if payments are being made at the beginning or end of the period. Use future value function 0 for payments made at the end of the period and 1 for payments made at the beginning of the period. In our example, type **1**.

NOTE ▼

The timing of the payment affects the amount of interest that will accrue.

9 Click **Finish**. Excel displays the results of the function in the selected cell. In our example, you would have **$115.07** after a year. ■

WHY WORRY?

The results of the function may be too large to fit in the column. If you see number signs (#) in the cell, make the column wider. See Part V for help.

Copying a Formula

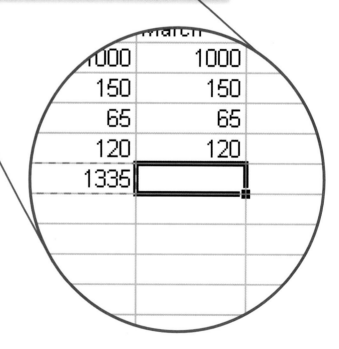

```
X Microsoft Excel - Book1.xls                                      _ 8 X
File   Edit   View   Insert   Format   Tools   Data   Window   Help   _ 8 X
```

	A	B	C	D	E	F	G	H	I
1	**Budget**			Budget	12-Sep	10:00			
2									
3									
4		January	February	March	Total				
5	Rent	1000	1000	1000	3000				
6	Car	150	150	150					
7	Telephone	65	65	65					
8	Electric	120	120	120					
9	Total	1335	1335						
10									
11	Avg Expen	333.75							
12									
13									
14									
15									
16									

```
Sheet1 / Sheet2 / Sheet3 / Sheet4 / Sheet5 / Sheet6
Select destination and press ENTER or choose Paste      Sum=0          CAPS NUM
Start   X Microsoft Excel - Boo...                                    3:59 PM
```

"Why would I do this?"

When you build your worksheet, you often use
the same formulas in more than one cell. You
already learned that you can use Excel's Copy
command to copy data; you can also create a
formula only once and then copy the formula
to other appropriate cells. You do not have to
go to each cell and enter the same basic
formula. For example, you might want to copy
a formula across a totals row so that you won't
have to type a formula to add up each row of
numbers.

1 On **Sheet1**, click cell **C9**, which contains the formula to add the numbers in C5:C8. You'll copy this formula to cell D9, which should contain a formula to add the numbers in cells D5:D8.

2 Click the **Copy** button on the Standard toolbar. A dashed marquee surrounds C9, the cell you are copying. The message **Select destination and press ENTER or choose Paste** appears in the status bar to remind you how to complete the task.

3 Click cell **D9**, where you want the copy of the formula in C9 to appear.

NOTE ▼

The formula in C9 uses *relative addressing*. Excel automatically adjusts the cell references when you copy the formula to reflect the cells at the new location. When you don't want Excel to adjust the formula you copy, set up the formula you want to copy using *absolute addressing*. See your Microsoft Excel User's Guide for help.

4 Click the **Paste** button on the Standard toolbar; then press **Esc** to remove the dashed marquee. Clicking the Paste button places a copy of the information you copied into the selected cell. The result of the formula appears in cell D9, and the formula bar contains the formula.

5 Using a "drag and drop" method, let's copy the formula in cell E5 to cells E6:E9. Click cell **E5** to select the cell that contains the formula you want to copy.

6 Move the mouse pointer to the fill handle in the lower right corner of cell E5 until the mouse pointer changes to a large black plus sign. Then drag the fill handle into cells **E6**, **E7**, **E8**, and **E9**. Excel fills the range E6:E9 with the formula from cell E5. Click any cell to remove the highlight— you might find it interesting to click cell **E6** and examine the formula in the formula bar. ■

Naming a Range

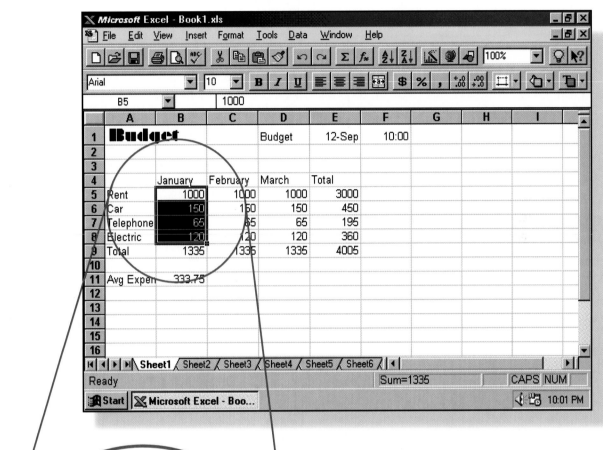

"Why would I do this?"

Naming ranges offers several advantages. Names are easier to remember than cell addresses. You can use range names in formulas. For example, suppose you use the SUM function to add a column of values, and the formula reads =SUM(B5:B8). If you were to give the range B5:B8 the name JANUARY, you could add that column with the function =SUM(JANUARY).

After you have created named ranges, you may want a list that tells you the name of each range and its cell addresses. Use Excel's Paste Name dialog box to create this list.

103

1 Select cells **B5**, **B6**, **B7**, and **B8**. This step selects the range you want to name—B5:B8.

> **NOTE** ▼
>
> You must start names with a letter. You can't use spaces. You can use lowercase or uppercase letters. Do not use a name that looks like a cell address (B15, for example).

2 Click the down arrow beside the name box in the formula bar. Excel opens the list box, highlights the cell address B5, and moves it to the left side of the name box.

3 Type **January**, the name you want to assign to this range. Press **Enter** to confirm the range name you want to assign—in this case, you'll assign **January** to cells B5 through B8. Excel adds the range name to the list of names in the name box.

4 Follow steps 1-3 to assign the name **February** to the range C5:C8 and **March** to range D5:D8.

> **NOTE** ▼
>
> Excel saves the name with the workbook when you save the workbook. When the range is selected, you see the range name in the name box in the formula bar.

5 Let's create a list, in the worksheet, of named ranges. Click cell **A13**. The list of range names will start in cell A13.

> **NOTE** ▼
>
> The list of names is two columns wide and as many rows long as there are names. Be careful not to place the table of names where it overwrites any data.

6 Click **Insert** in the menu bar, select **Name**, and then click **Paste** to open the Paste Name dialog box.

7 Click the **Paste List** button. Then click any cell to deselect the range. Excel inserts the two-column table in a range beginning with cell A13. The first column lists the range names in alphabetical order; the second column lists the range coordinates for each name. ▪

WHY WORRY?

To delete a range name, select the **Insert**, **Name**, **Define** command, highlight the name in the **Names in Workbook** list box, and click **Delete**. Then click **OK**.

PART IV
Managing Files

Now that you've learned the basics on starting Excel, moving around, entering information, and performing math-related activities, it's time to learn how to save your work. In fact, it's time to learn about managing workbook files in Excel. In this part, you learn how to save your work, abandon a workbook that you don't want to save, create a new workbook, open a workbook, find a workbook, close a workbook, and rename the sheets in a workbook. You might already be familiar with using windows inside applications such as Excel. If you want to skip the first part of this section, feel free to do so, but be sure to read the tasks on how to find a workbook and rename sheets within a workbook.

Excel does not automatically save your work, so you should save every five or ten minutes. If you don't save your work, you could lose it. Suppose that you have been working on a worksheet for a few hours and your power goes off unexpectedly—an air conditioning repairman at your office shorts out the power, a thunderstorm hits, or something else causes a power loss. If you haven't saved, you lose all your hard work. Of course, you should also make backup copies on floppy disks from time to time of important worksheets.

Saving a file that you previously saved is slightly different from saving a newly created workbook. When you save a workbook you saved before, you save the current version on-screen and overwrite the original version on disk. This means you always have the most current version of your file stored on disk.

If you want to keep both versions—the on-screen version and the original—you can use the File, Save As command to save the on-screen version with a different name. Saving a file with a new name gives you two copies of the same worksheet with differences in their data. When you save a file with a new name, you also can save the file in a different directory or drive.

Saving a workbook does not remove it from the screen. To remove a workbook from the screen, you must close the workbook. Whether you've saved a workbook or not, you can close it using the File, Close command.

You can open more than one workbook at a time. For example, you might have two separate workbooks that contain related information. While using one workbook, you can view the information in another, or even copy information from one workbook to the other. Having both workbooks open and in view makes this possible. The number of workbooks you can open depends on the amount of memory available in your computer.

When you open several workbooks, they can overlap—essentially hiding workbooks beneath other workbooks. Excel lets you rearrange the workbooks so that some part of each workbook is visible. Arranging the open windows into smaller windows of similar sizes is one of several arrangement options you can choose from. This is called *tiling windows*. Tiling windows is handy when you want to compare the figures in two workbooks side by side. You can use the Window, Arrange Tiles command to arrange the windows in the tiled effect. If you want to display one workbook after you are finished using the tiled window arrangement, close the workbooks you do not want displayed and select the Window, Arrange All command. The workbook you want to display fills the screen.

Although Windows 95 lets you use long file names so that you can provide meaningful names for your workbook files, sometimes you simply forget where you stored certain information. Excel lets you search for a workbook using any search criteria. For example, you can find a workbook using its file name, disk, or directory as search criteria.

As you learned earlier, a new Excel workbook has 16 sheets and can contain as many as 255 sheets (depending on your computer's available memory). The sheets are named Sheet1 through Sheet16. You can rename sheets to clearly identify the contents of each sheet. For example, you can rename Sheet1 to QTR 1, Sheet2 to QTR 2, and so on.

In this part, you are introduced to the essential file management skills that you will need in order to work with files in Excel.

Saving a Workbook

"Why would I do this?"

Until you save the workbook, your data is not
stored on a disk. You can lose your data if
something happens, such as a power loss. Once
you save a workbook, you can retrieve it from
the disk when you need the workbook again.
Because Excel doesn't automatically save for
you, always save your work every five or ten
minutes and at the end of a work session. Then
close the workbook if you want to clear the
screen. Excel also lets you close a previously
saved workbook without saving the changes.

1 Click the **Save** button on the Standard toolbar, which selects the Save command located on the File menu. The first time you save the workbook, Excel displays the Save As dialog box. Type a name for your workbook that means something to you in the **File Name** text box. In our example, **Budget 1995** is a meaningful name.

2 Click **Save**. Excel redisplays the workbook. The file name, **Budget 1995.xls**, appears in the title bar. ■

WHY WORRY?

If you type a file name that already exists, Excel displays an alert box that asks **Replace existing file?**. Click **Cancel** to return to the Save As dialog box and then type a new name.

NOTE ▼

With Windows 95's new "long names" convention, you are no longer limited to eight characters. And, file names can include spaces. Also, you don't need to worry about an extension—by default, Excel will save your workbook as an Excel file and assign the extension automatically for you.

Closing a Workbook

"Why would I do this?"

When you no longer want to work with a workbook, you can use the File, Close command to close the workbook. Closing the workbook removes it from your screen, but if you save the workbook it will be available on disk. You can use the Open button on the Standard toolbar to reopen a closed workbook. Or, if you want to start a new workbook, use the New Workbook button on the Standard toolbar.

1 Click **File** in the menu bar. Excel opens the File menu.

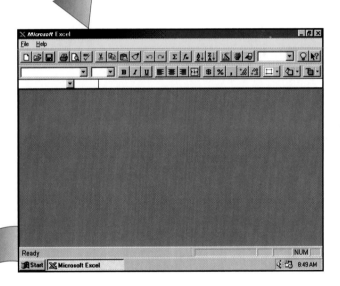

> **NOTE** ▼
>
> You can also click the Close (X) box in the upper right corner of the workbook window to close a workbook. Make sure you click the Close box of the lower set of three icons—the one for the workbook window. The upper Close box closes the program, not just the workbook.

2 Click the **Close** command. If you saved the file immediately before choosing the File, Close command, Excel closes the workbook. You see just the toolbars and two menu options: File and Help. From here, you can open a workbook or create a new workbook.

3 If you made changes, Excel displays an alert box that reminds you to save them. Choose **Yes** to save the changes and close the workbook. If you made changes you don't want to save, choose **No** to ignore the changes and close the workbook. ■

> **WHY WORRY?**
>
> If you need to make more changes before closing, click **Cancel**. Excel takes you back to the workbook.

TASK 33
Creating a New Workbook

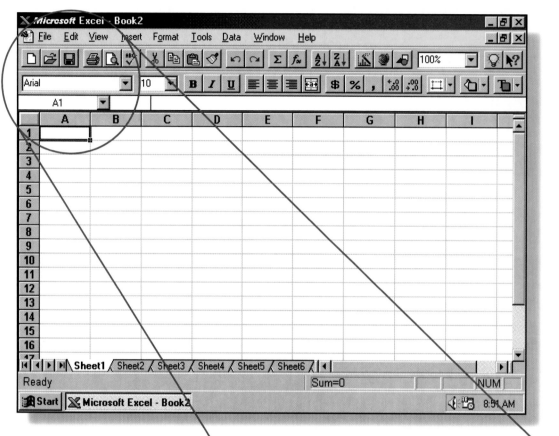

"Why would I do this?"

Excel presents a new, blank workbook when you first start the program. You can create another new workbook at any time. Perhaps you have closed and saved the active workbook and want to begin a new one.

In this task you'll create a new workbook and see how it works. Then you'll close the new workbook.

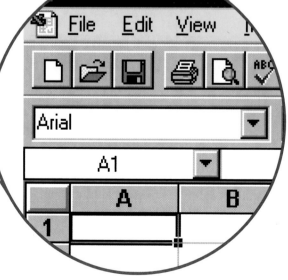

1 Click the **New Workbook** button on the Standard toolbar. Clicking the New Workbook button selects the File, New command. A blank workbook appears on-screen. This workbook is titled **Book2** (the number varies depending on the number of workbooks you have open).

NOTE ▼

When you start Excel, the program automatically displays a blank workbook. You don't have to use the File, New command in this case.

2 Click **File** in the menu bar and then click **Close** to abandon the new workbook. Excel closes the workbook. As you can see, there are two menu options left: File and Help. In the next task, you open a workbook. ■

Opening a Workbook

"Why would I do this?"

After you save and close a workbook, you can view it again to make changes to it later. Or perhaps you want to examine the sample workbooks that came with Excel. The sample workbooks are stored in Excel's EXAMPLES folder.

1 Suppose you want to work with the Budget 1995 file again. Click the **Open** button on the Standard toolbar; this selects the File, Open command. You see the Open dialog box.

NOTE ▼

The Open dialog box also contains the Look In list. If the file is stored in a different directory, open the **Look In** list box and navigate to the folder that contains the file.

2 Highlight the file you want to open. In our example, highlight **Budget 1995.xls**. Then, either click the **Open** button or double-click the file name. Excel opens the workbook and displays it on-screen. The file name appears in the title bar. ■

WHY WORRY?

If you open the wrong workbook, close the workbook (**File**, **Close**) and try again.

Finding a Workbook

"Why would I do this?"

From the Open dialog box, you can search for a single file or group of files based on search criteria you specify. When Excel finds the files, you can perform a variety of operations such as preview, print, or delete files. This feature is handy when you can't remember the name of a file that contains certain information. Let's search for all files containing the word **January**.

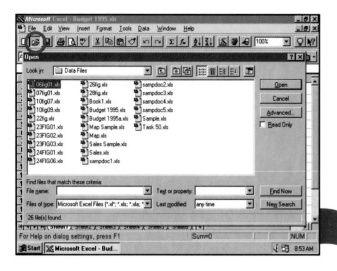

1 Click the **Open** button on the Standard toolbar to select the File, Open command. Excel displays the Open dialog box.

2 Navigate to the folder you want to search by clicking the arrow next to the **Look in** list box.

NOTE

By clicking the Advanced button, you can specify advanced search criteria and save search criteria.

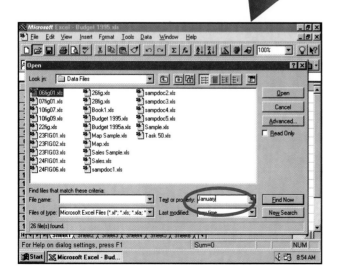

3 Click in the **Text or property** box in the lower right corner of the Open dialog box and type **January**. Notice that Excel searches for all Microsoft Excel files.

4 Click the **Find Now** button. Excel searches the *contents* of the files in the current folder for the word **January** and displays, in the list, only those that meet the search criteria.

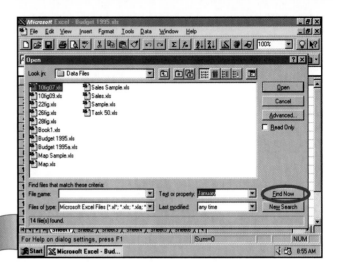

5 To open, print, or delete a file that met the search criteria, highlight the file. Then, point the mouse pointer at the highlighted file, open the shortcut menu by clicking the right mouse button, and select your choice. ■

NOTE ▼

To preview a file's contents, click the **Preview** button at the upper right edge of the Open dialog box.

WHY WORRY?

To redisplay all the files in the folder, remove the search criteria and click the **Find Now** button again.

Renaming
Sheets

"Why would I do this?"

You can rename sheets in a workbook. This feature lets you change the name of a sheet without altering its contents. Renaming sheets is especially useful if you want to clearly label each sheet in a workbook that contains many worksheets. For example, if you create an annual budget, you can name each sheet tab with January, February, and so on, and then name the final sheet Summary.

1 Double-click the **Sheet1** tab. Double-clicking the sheet tab displays the Rename Sheet dialog box. The insertion point is in the Name text box.

2 Type the name you want to give the sheet, such as **QTR 1** in our example. As a rule, you can use a maximum of 31 characters, including spaces.

3 Click **OK**. The new sheet name appears on the first sheet tab.

4 Repeat steps 1-3 to rename **Sheet2** with the name **Qtr 2**, **Sheet3** with the name **Invoice**, **Sheet4** with the name **Balance**, and **Sheet5** with the name **Log**.

5 Click the **Qtr 1** tab to return to the first worksheet. Then click the **Save** button on the Standard toolbar to save the file. ■

WHY WORRY?

If you rename the wrong tab, just follow the procedure again, resupplying the tab's original name. Then, start over and rename the correct tab.

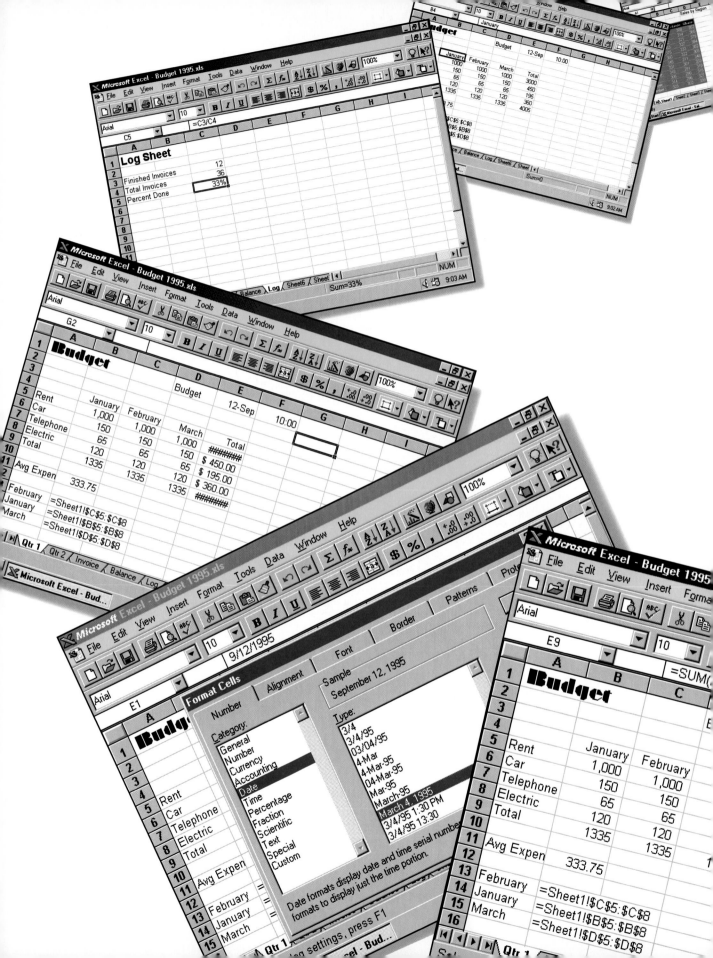

PART V

Formatting the Worksheet

By formatting the worksheet, you change the appearance of data on your worksheet. With Excel's formatting tools, you can make your worksheet more attractive and readable. In this part you first learn how to automatically format ranges in your worksheet. Then, if you prefer to exercise greater control over the appearance of the worksheet, you can use the techniques for centering and right-aligning data in a cell, displaying dollar signs, commas, and percent signs, changing the number of decimal places, and formatting a date and a time. You also learn how to copy formats with Excel's Format Painter button, change column width, format individual words, shade cells, add borders, and turn off gridlines.

You can align data in a cell to the left, center, or right. The default alignment is General. *General alignment* means that numbers are right-aligned and text is left-aligned.

There will be many times you will format cells that don't have numbers in them yet. For example, in your workbook, on the Qtr 2 sheet, the cells contain the figures for Rent, Food, Telephone, Car, and Total for the second quarter. You can format those cells with commas even though the cells don't contain numbers yet. When numbers are entered into those cells, they automatically appear with commas.

Excel lets you change the width of any column and the height of any row. You can use the AutoFit feature to quickly change the width of any column. Just double-click the line next to the column letter in the column you want to adjust. Excel automatically changes the width of the column based on the longest entry in that column. If you want to reset the column width to the original setting, choose the Format, Column, Standard Width command.

A *font* is a particular typeface, and Excel allows you to establish the font's size. There are various fonts and font sizes displayed in the Formatting toolbar. You can use the fonts provided by Excel as well as fonts designed especially for your printer. If Excel does not have a screen version of the printer font you select, it substitutes a font. When Excel makes a substitution, the printout looks different from the screen.

You can apply fonts to a single cell or a range of cells. You can enhance fonts by using boldface type, italics, or underscore, and Excel also allows you to change font colors. Varying the font appearance and colors to emphasize data makes your worksheet more attractive. The Font Color button on the Formatting toolbar lets you change font colors in a snap. Of course, you must have a color monitor and a color printer to benefit from changing font colors.

In Excel, you can apply preset formats to selected data on a worksheet with the AutoFormat command. Generally, you apply one format at a time to a selected range. However, now you can apply a collection of formats supplied by Excel all at once. The formats help you create professional-looking financial reports, lists, and large tables.

One of the best ways to enhance the appearance of a worksheet is to add borders to the data on the worksheet. You can use the Borders button on the Formatting toolbar to add boxes around cells and ranges, and you can add emphasis lines anywhere on the worksheet.

Another way to change the overall worksheet display is to remove the gridlines that separate the cells in the worksheet. Your worksheet looks cleaner when you turn off the gridlines.

In this section, you learn some of the most important formatting operations you need for changing the appearance and layout of your worksheets.

Automatically Formatting a Range

```
X Microsoft Excel - Sales.xls                                    _ 8 X
File  Edit  View  Insert  Format  Tools  Data  Window  Help      _ 8 X
```

	A	B	C	D	E	F	G	H	I	J
1				Sales by Region						
2										
3		*Tampa*	*Orlando*	*Miami*						
4	January	332	308	352						
5	February	342	314	365						
6	March	352	321	379						
7	April	363	327	394						
8	May	375	333	382						
9	June	360	322	365						
10	July	345	311	348						
11	August	331	301	333						
12	September	318	291	318						
13	October	305	290	315						
14	November	314	296	327						
15	December	323	302	339						
16										

```
Sheet1  Sheet2  Sheet3  Sheet4  Sheet5  Sheet6
Ready                              Sum=0                    NUM
Start  X Microsoft Excel - Sal...
```

	Tampa	*Orla...*
January	332	3...
February	342	31...
March	352	32...
April	363	32...
May	375	3...
June	360	
	345	

"Why would I do this?"

AutoFormatting is the easiest way to apply formatting to a table-like range in your worksheet. You choose from a group of predefined formats and Excel applies them to the specified range. These formats include many of the options we'll be discussing individually in this section and quickly change the appearance of data in a table. You'll use the options we discuss later to format individual cells or small groups of cells.

Open a new worksheet by clicking the **New** button on the Standard toolbar. Then, enter the data you see in the figure next to this step.

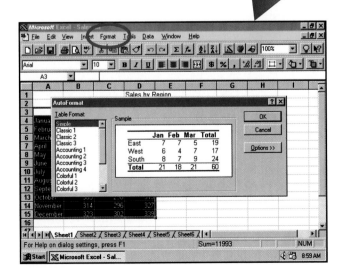

Select cells **A3:D15**. This is the range you want Excel to automatically format.

Click **Format** and then click **AutoFormat** to open the AutoFormat dialog box.

4 To preview the possible formats for your table, click an option in the Table Format list on the left side of the dialog box and watch the Sample box change to reflect the formatting for that option. For example, click **Colorful 1**. You can preview as many formats as you want without applying any of them.

5 To apply formatting, click the option you want to apply and choose **OK**. In our example, let's select a different format than the one we previewed. Let's select **Classic 2**. ■

WHY WORRY?

If you don't like the results of Auto-Formatting, click the **Undo** tool on the Standard toolbar. Or, reopen the AutoFormat dialog box and choose **None** from the **Table Format** list.

Aligning Text

"Why would I do this?"

When you enter data into a cell, numbers, dates, and times automatically align with the right side of the cell. Text aligns with the left side of the cell. You can change the alignment of information at any time. For instance, you might want to fine-tune the appearance of column headings across columns. You can center headings across the columns or you can right-align the headings to line them up with the numbers that are right-aligned.

133

1 In the Budget worksheet, hold down the mouse button and drag the mouse to select cells **B4**, **C4**, **D4**, and **E4**—the range you want to right-align. Notice that these entries are left-aligned.

2 Click the **Align Right** button on the Formatting toolbar. Then click any cell to deselect the range. Excel right-aligns the contents of each cell in the range. ∎

WHY WORRY?

To undo the most recent alignment change, click the **Undo** button on the Standard toolbar.

NOTE ▼

While aligning is used primarily for text entries, you can align numbers. But, be sure *not* to align numbers if you want Excel to use the numbers in a formula. If you align numbers left or center, Excel does not recognize the numbers as values and considers them text.

Displaying Dollar Signs, Commas, and Percent Signs

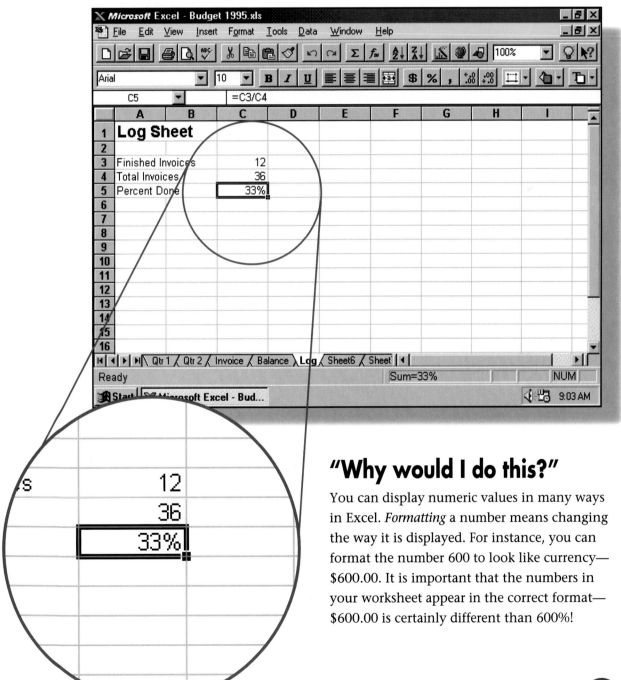

"Why would I do this?"

You can display numeric values in many ways in Excel. *Formatting* a number means changing the way it is displayed. For instance, you can format the number 600 to look like currency— $600.00. It is important that the numbers in your worksheet appear in the correct format— $600.00 is certainly different than 600%!

1 In the Budget worksheet, hold down the mouse button and drag the mouse to select cells **E5** to **E9**, the range in which you want to display dollar signs.

2 Click the **Currency Style** button on the Formatting toolbar. Then click any cell to deselect the range. Clicking the Currency Style button tells Excel to display dollar signs, commas, and two decimal places.

NOTE ▼

If you see number signs (#) in the column, the entry is too long to fit in the column. You must change the column width. Later in this section, you'll learn how to make the column wider.

3 Hold down the mouse button and drag the mouse to select cells **B5** to **D8**, the range in which you want to display commas.

4 Click the **Comma Style** button on the Formatting toolbar. Then click any cell to deselect the range. Clicking the Comma Style button tells Excel to display commas and two decimal places.

5 Click the **Log** sheet tab to move to the Log worksheet. Then click cell **C5** to select cell C5, in which you want to display a percent sign.

6 Click the **Percent Style** button on the Formatting toolbar to tell Excel to display percent signs and zero decimal places. ■

WHY WORRY?

To undo the most recent formatting change, click the **Undo** button on the Standard toolbar.

Specifying Decimal Places

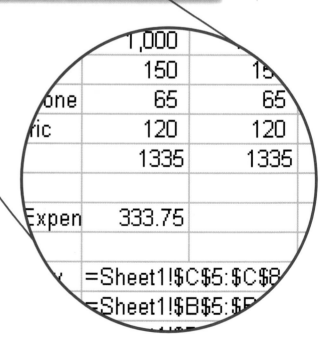

"Why would I do this?"

Decimal places are often added to numbers when you change the format of numbers. For example, Excel assumes you want two decimal places when you change the format to Currency. However, sometimes you don't want any decimal places, or you want a different number of decimal places than what's displayed. For example, if your Currency numbers aren't going to have cents, then you don't need to display two decimal places.

1 Click the **Qtr 1** sheet tab of the Budget worksheet. Then hold down the mouse button and drag the mouse to select cells **B5** to **D8**. This step selects the range B5:D8 in which you want to specify decimal places.

2 Click the **Decrease Decimal** button on the Formatting toolbar twice. Each time you click the Decrease Decimal button, Excel moves the decimal point one place to the right. Click any cell to deselect the range. ■

NOTE ▼

If you select zero decimal places, Excel rounds the values to fit this format. If you enter 7.5 in a cell, Excel rounds to 8 when formatting to zero decimal places.

WHY WORRY?

To undo the most recent formatting change, click the **Undo** button on the Standard toolbar.

Changing Date and Time Formats

"Why would I do this?"

In Excel, you can enter dates in several different ways so that Excel accepts the date and displays it in a particular format. If you like, you can change the way Excel displays the date and the time. For instance, you might prefer 9/12/1995 or September 12, 1995. Excel assumes the 24-hour time format unless you enter an a.m. or p.m. designation. The time 10:00 in cell E1 in your budget might be clearer as 10:00 AM.

1 Select cell **E1** in the **Qtr 1** sheet. Then click the right mouse button to select the cell you want to format and to display the shortcut menu.

2 Click **Format Cells**. Excel displays Number options in the Format Cells dialog box. Because the cell is already formatted as a date, the Date Category is selected and date formats appear in the Type list.

3 Click **March 4, 1994** from the Type list. A sample appears at the top of the dialog box and uses the value in the selected cell to preview the format.

4 Click **OK** to confirm the format choice. Excel displays the date in the new format, but you can't see it because the new format is too wide for the cell. You'll learn how to change the column width in a task later in this part. Next, you change the time format.

5 Select cell **F1**—the time entry you want to format.

6 Press **Ctrl+1** (use the 1 above the typing keys, not on the numeric keypad) to select the Format, Cells command. Excel opens the Format Cells dialog box and displays Number options in the dialog box. The current time format is selected. Because the cell is already formatted as a time, the Time Category is selected and time formats appear in the Type list.

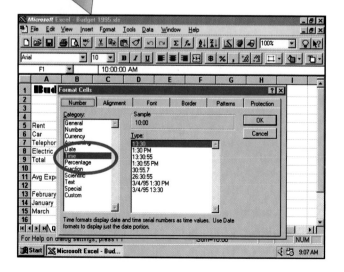

Click **1:30 PM**. This format tells Excel to display the time using a 12-hour clock and include **AM** or **PM** when displaying the time. A sample appears at the top of the dialog box.

Click **OK** to confirm the format choice. Excel displays the time in the new format—**10:00 AM**. ■

NOTE ▼

If you see number signs (#) in the column, the entry is too long to fit in the column. You must change the column width (see a task later in this part).

WHY WORRY?

To undo the most recent formatting change, click the **Undo** button on the Standard toolbar.

Copying Formats

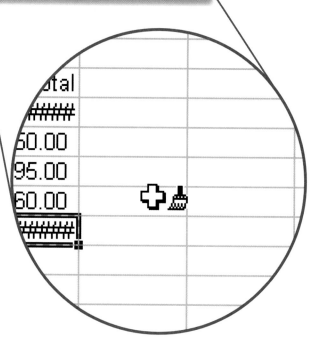

"Why would I do this?"

When the label or the format of a number appears the way you want it, you don't have to repeat the formatting process for the rest of the labels or numbers you want to change. A quick way to copy the formatting of one label or number to all the others that must match it is to use the Format Painter button.

1 Click cell **E9** to select the cell that has the formats you want to copy. This cell has the Currency format.

2 Click the **Format Painter** button on the Standard toolbar. This selects the Copy and Paste Format commands. A dashed copy marquee surrounds cell E9.

NOTE

The mouse pointer changes to a white cross with a paintbrush. The cross and paintbrush indicate you are copying formats.

3 Move the mouse anywhere over the active cell and drag the mouse pointer across the cells **B9**, **C9**, and **D9**. When you release the mouse button, Excel copies the formats of cell E9 to B9:D9. Click any cell to deselect the range. ■

WHY WORRY?

To undo the most recent formatting change, click the **Undo** button on the Standard toolbar.

TASK 43
Changing Column Width

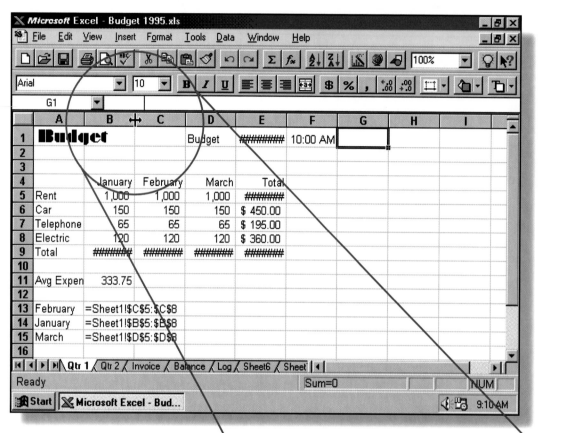

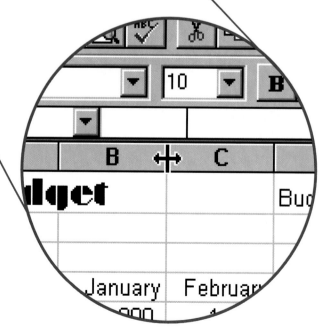

"Why would I do this?"

Number signs (#) in a cell indicate that the column is not wide enough to display the results of the formula. Often, the formatting (and the selected font) makes the entry longer than the default column width. For example, $3,000 is only six characters, but if you format the number as currency with two decimal places, the number appears as $3,000.00. This number requires nine spaces.

1 Move the mouse pointer into the column header area (where the column letters appear) onto the line to the right of the column you want to widen. In our example, move the mouse point onto the line that separates column **B** from column **C** so that you can widen column B. The mouse pointer changes to a two-headed arrow attached to a vertical black bar.

2 Hold down the mouse button. Drag the mouse a small amount to the right to make the column wider. Excel widens the column. If you still see number signs (#), widen the column more.

WHY WORRY?

If you drag to the left, you make the column narrower.

3 Let's use the AutoFit feature to adjust the width of column E. Place the mouse pointer in the column header area (where you see the letters of the columns), on the line on the right side of the column that you want to adjust—in this case, to the right of column **E**.

4 Double-click the line to the right of Column **E**. Double-clicking on the right side of the column automatically adjusts the width of the column based on the longest entry in the column. Excel calls this feature "AutoFit."

5 Repeat Steps 3 and 4 for Columns **C** and **D** so that you can see all the numbers in the worksheet. ■

Changing and Enhancing Fonts

"Why would I do this?"

To bring attention to important words and numbers in a worksheet, you can change the font, font size, font style, and font color. For example, you can change the font for text in the body of your worksheet to New Times Roman in order to make reading easier. In addition, you can specify styles such as bold, italic, and underline to emphasize significant words and numbers.

1 Select cell **A1** to select the title of the worksheet—the text you want to change.

NOTE ▼

Desktop publishing guidelines suggest that you use sans serif fonts such as Arial for headlines and titles, and serif fonts such as New Times Roman for text in paragraphs and in the body of the worksheet. *Sans serif* fonts do not contain tails on the letters, while *serif* fonts do contain tails. The text in the steps appears in a serif font—note the lines at the bottom of letters such as l, m, n, or f.

2 Click the down arrow next to the **Font** box on the Formatting toolbar. This step displays the list of fonts.

NOTE ▼

The fonts in the list can vary, depending on the type of printer you have and the fonts installed.

3 Click any font in the list to change the font for the text in the selected range. I chose **Courier** because most computers or printers have Courier. The text appears in the new font.

Next, you change the font size to a larger font to emphasize it more. With cell **A1** selected, click the down arrow next to the **Font Size** box on the Formatting toolbar to display the list of font sizes.

NOTE

The font sizes in the list can vary, depending on the type of printer you have and the selected font.

5 Click a larger font size (a higher number) to change the font size for the title. I chose **15**. Next, bring more attention to the title by applying bold to it.

6 Click the **Bold** button on the Formatting toolbar. Then click any cell to move the cell pointer out of the way so that you can easily see the changes. Clicking the Bold button applies bold to the selected cells—in this case, A1.

7 Select cells **B4:E4**. Then click the **Italics** button on the Formatting toolbar. Click any cell to deselect the range and easily see the changes. Clicking the Italics button italicizes the data in the selected cells—in this case, B4:E4.

8 To remove the italics style, select cells **B4:E4**, and then click the **Italics** button on the Formatting toolbar. Click any cell to deselect the range and see the changes. ■

WHY WORRY?

To undo any of these changes, immediately click the **Undo** button.

Adding Cell Tips

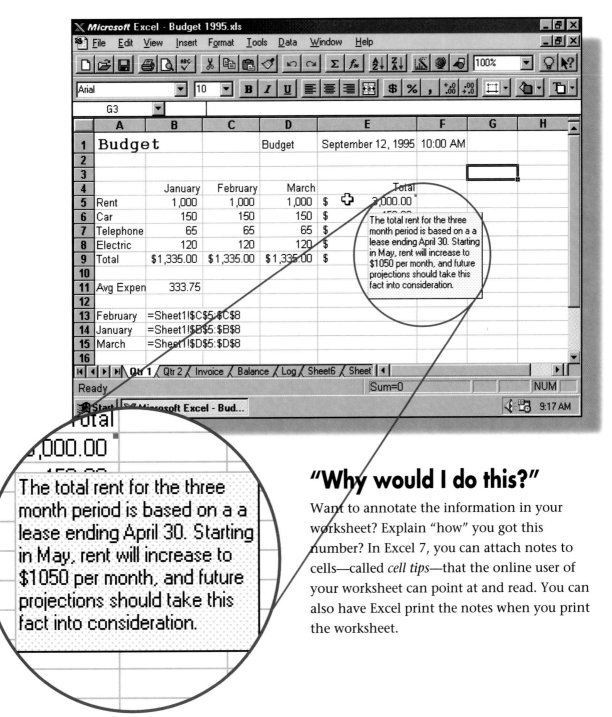

"Why would I do this?"

Want to annotate the information in your worksheet? Explain "how" you got this number? In Excel 7, you can attach notes to cells—called *cell tips*—that the online user of your worksheet can point at and read. You can also have Excel print the notes when you print the worksheet.

1 Click cell **E5**, where we'll place an explanatory note about rent.

2 Open the **Insert** menu and choose the **Note** command. Excel displays the Cell Note dialog box. The insertion point appears in the Text Note box.

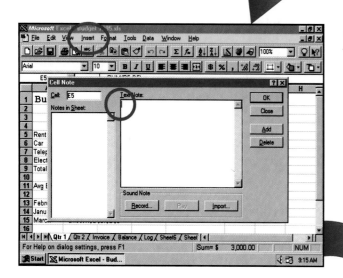

NOTE ▼

When you print cell notes, Excel does not identify the cell to which the note is attached. Therefore, it is wise for you to include in your explanation some description that identifies for the reader the cell to which the note refers.

3 Type the text you want to attach to the current cell. In our example, type: **The total rent for the three month period is based on a lease ending April 30. Starting in May, rent will increase to $1050 per month, and future projections should take this fact into consideration**.

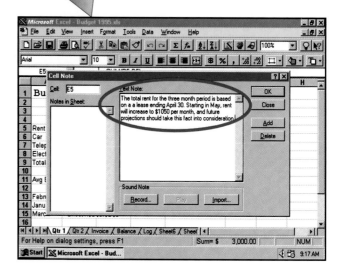

4 Click the **Add** button. Excel adds a reference in the Notes in Sheet list box that identifies the cell to which the note will be attached.

5 Click **OK**. Then, click in any cell other than E5. Excel closes the dialog box and after you move the cell pointer, you see a red dot in the upper right corner of E5. This red dot indicates that a cell tip is associated with cell E5.

6 To see the cell tip, slide the mouse pointer over any cell containing a red dot in the upper right corner—in this case, cell **E5**. Excel displays the cell tip.

155

7 To print cell tips, click in the sheet containing the cell tip—in this case **Qtr 1**. Then click **File** in the menu bar and then click the **Page Setup** command. You'll see the Page Setup dialog box with four tabs in it.

8 Click the **Sheet** tab and place a check in the **Notes** check box. ∎

NOTE ▼

After you save the Page Setup settings, when you print the sheet, Excel will print the notes on a separate page.

WHY WORRY?

To remove a note from a worksheet, reopen the Cell Notes dialog box (click **Insert** and then **Note**). In the Cell Notes dialog box, highlight the note you want to remove in the **Notes in Sheet** list box and then click the **Delete** button.

Shading Cells

"Why would I do this?"

You can shade cells to draw attention to certain text or numbers in your worksheet. You might want to shade a high or low sales figure, an average, or a grand total.

1 Click cell **B11**. This is the cell you want to shade.

2 Click the down arrow next to the **Color** button on the Formatting toolbar to display a color palette.

3 In the first row of the palette, click the third color from the left—red. Then click any cell to move the pointer and see the results better. On-screen, you see the shading of cell B11 change. ■

WHY WORRY?

To remove the shading, immediately click the **Undo** button on the Standard toolbar.

Adding Borders

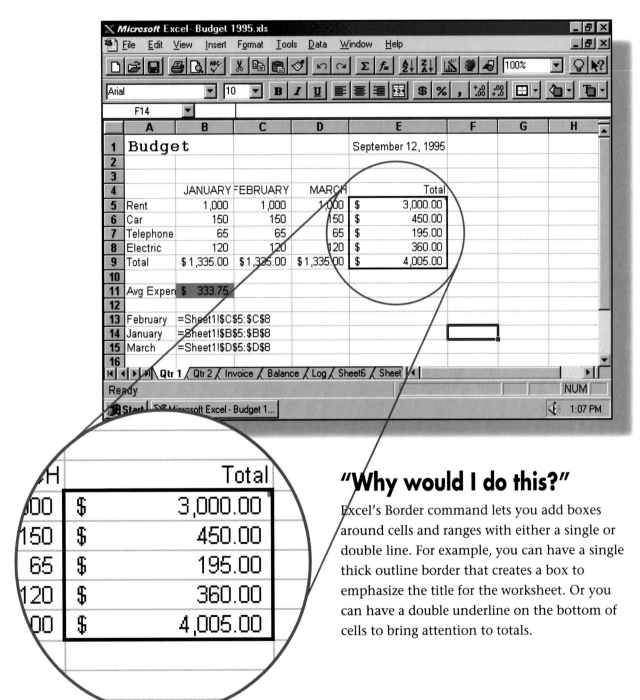

"Why would I do this?"

Excel's Border command lets you add boxes around cells and ranges with either a single or double line. For example, you can have a single thick outline border that creates a box to emphasize the title for the worksheet. Or you can have a double underline on the bottom of cells to bring attention to totals.

1 Select cells **E5** to **E9** to select the range you want to outline—E5:E9.

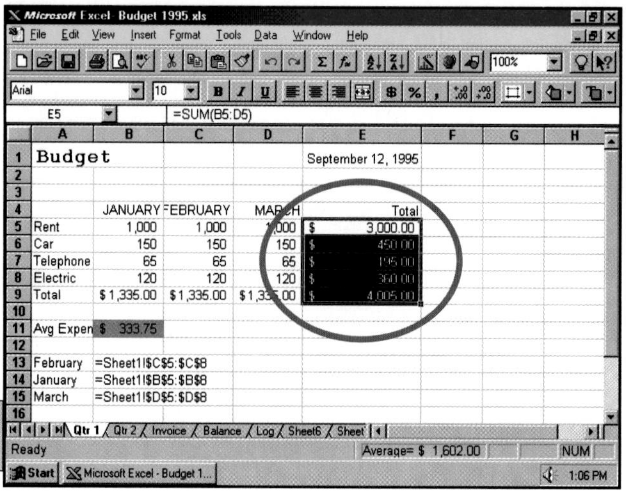

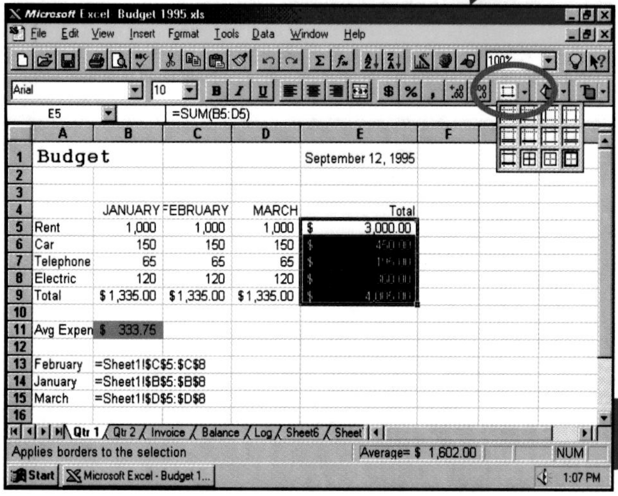

2 Click the down arrow next to the **Borders** button on the Formatting toolbar to display a palette of border samples.

NOTE ▼

Borders can be hard to see because the gridlines are displayed on-screen.

3 Now let's tell Excel to outline the edges of the range with a thick single line. In the last column of the palette, click the last border sample. Then click any other cell to deselect the range so you can see the outline better. ■

WHY WORRY?

To remove the outline, immediately click the **Undo** button on the Standard toolbar.

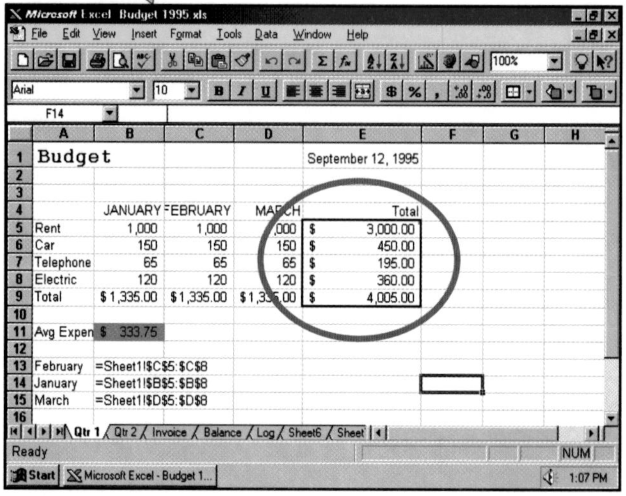

Turning Off Gridlines

"Why would I do this?"

Another way to make your worksheet look more attractive is to turn off the gridlines that separate the cells in the worksheet. Your worksheet seems cleaner on the white background without the grids. You might want to turn off gridlines in your worksheets to see how the data looks when printed on white paper.

1 Click **Tools** in the menu bar, and then click **Options**. Now click the **View** tab. Excel displays the View options in the Options dialog box.

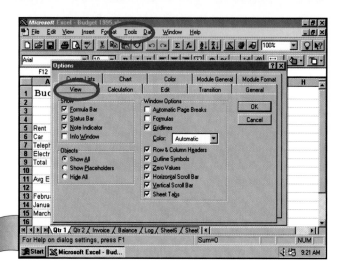

2 Click the check box next to **Gridlines** in the Window Options area to remove the check mark from the check box and deselect the Gridlines option.

WHY WORRY?

If you change your mind and you want to turn on the gridlines again, click the check box next to **Gridlines** to select the Gridlines option in the Options dialog box.

3 Click **OK** to confirm your choice. The gridlines no longer appear in the worksheet. Now click the **Save** button on the Standard toolbar to save the file. ■

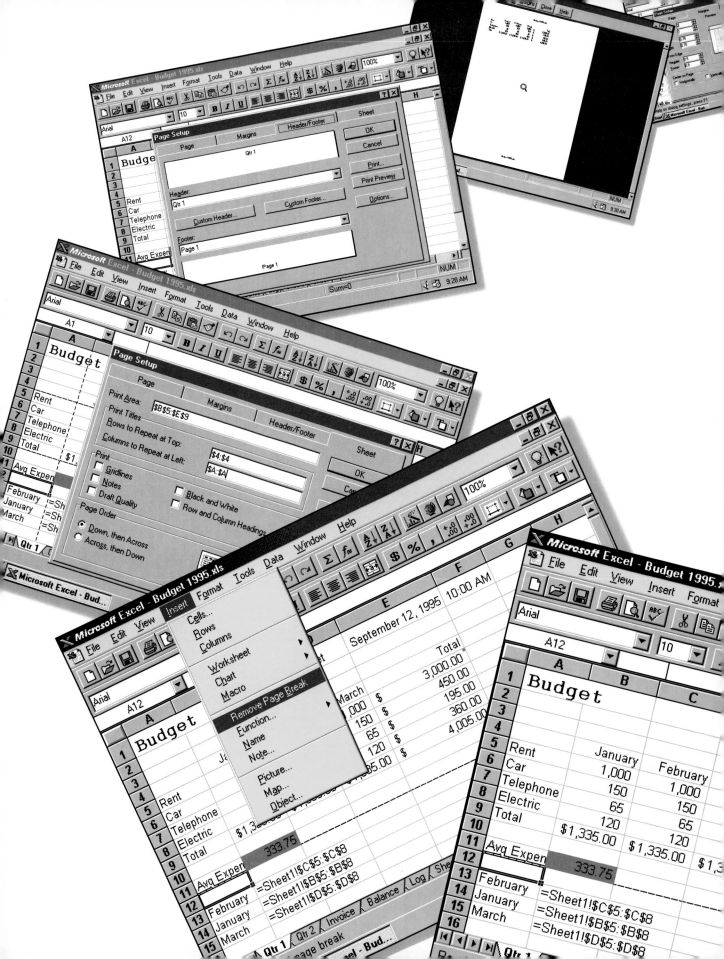

PART VI

Printing the Worksheet

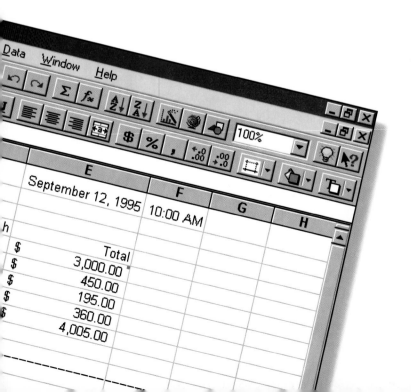

I n Excel, you can print your worksheets using a basic printing procedure or you can enhance the printout using several print options. It is fairly simple to print a worksheet in Excel.

First, you set up the format for your printout. You can insert manual page breaks in your worksheet to split the worksheet into two or more pages. Otherwise, Excel automatically sets the page breaks. When you set manual page breaks, you set horizontal or vertical page breaks by selecting the row below or the column to the right of where you want the page break to appear. Manual page breaks override automatic page breaks and remain on the worksheet until you remove them. Inserting new manual page breaks does not change existing manual page breaks; it just adds to them.

You will find most print options in the Page Setup dialog box. In Excel for Windows 95, the Page Setup dialog box contains four types of options: Page, Margins, Header/ Footer, and Sheet. You can move from one set of options to another by clicking the appropriate tab in the Page Setup dialog box.

There are several important Sheet options you might find useful. You can tell Excel what part of the worksheet you want to print using the Print Area option. For large worksheets, you might want to print headings for each column at the top of each page with the Rows to Repeat at Top option. You can print headings for each row at the left side of each page with the Columns to Repeat at Left option.

With Excel's Print Preview feature, you can review the appearance of the worksheet before you print the final product. The first page of the worksheet appears as a reduced image in the Print Preview screen. However, you can use the Zoom feature in Print Preview to magnify the view. This allows you to inspect the printout more closely. Then, when you click the Zoom button again, Excel reduces the view to a smaller image again. You can also change the margins and page setup and start printing from the Preview window. See your Microsoft Excel documentation for complete information.

The first time you use your printer with Excel, it is a good idea to check the Setup options. Excel can use the options and capabilities that are available with each printer. Often, you will need to provide more details about your printer so that Excel knows the capabilities available. If you want to specify details about your printer, choose the File, Print command. From within the Print dialog box, choose Properties. Then you can confirm that Excel will be printing to the correct printer, or you can switch to a different printer.

The Page and Margins options in the Page Setup dialog box control print enhancements such as orientation, margins, and the size of the paper you use. The default print orientation is Portrait, which means that the worksheet prints vertically on the paper. You can choose Landscape to print the worksheet sideways or horizontally on the paper. If the worksheet is too wide, you can try decreasing the widths of some cells if possible.

If the worksheet is still too large to print on one page, you can change the top, bottom, left, and right margins. You also might consider reducing the printout using the Adjust To option in the Page Setup dialog box. Some printers will let you reduce or enlarge the printout as it prints. Although 100 percent is normal size, you can enter the desired reduction or enlargement percentage you want.

The Fit To option prints the worksheet at full size to fit the size of the page. You can enter the number of pages in the Page(s) Wide By and the Tall text boxes to specify the document's width and height. This is useful for printing graphics and charts. This option may not be available on all printers, and you may need to experiment with all the print options until you get the results you want.

Excel lets you add headers and footers to print information at the top and bottom of every page of the printout. You can choose the headers and footers suggested by Excel, or you can include any text plus special commands to control the appearance of the header or footer.

It is a good idea to save your worksheets before printing—just in case a printer error or other problem occurs. This ensures that you won't lose any work since the last time you saved the worksheet. You learn how to print your worksheet from the Page Setup dialog box. But if you already set up your print options and you're back viewing the worksheet, you can just click the Print button on the Standard toolbar to print your worksheet. If, however, you want to print only a portion of the workbook, use Excel's Print dialog box. The Print dialog box lets you print some or all the sheets within a workbook, a range of pages, and multiple copies of the printout.

This part introduces you to the basics of printing the worksheet. With some experimentation and practice, you will be able to create some very interesting printed results.

TASK 49

Inserting and Removing Page Breaks

Microsoft Excel - Budget 1995.xls

File   Edit   View   Insert   Format   Tools   Data   Window   Help

Arial   10   **B** *I* U

A12

	A	B	C	D	E	F	G	H
1	**Budget**			Budget	September 12, 1995	10:00 AM		
2								
3								
4		January	February	March	Total			
5	Rent	1,000	1,000	1,000	$ 3,000.00			
6	Car	150	150	150	$ 450.00			
7	Telephone	65	65	65	$ 195.00			
8	Electric	120	120	120	$ 360.00			
9	Total	$1,335.00	$1,335.00	$1,335.00	$ 4,005.00			
10								
11	Avg Expen	333.75						
12								
13	February	=Sheet1!$C$5:$C$8						
14	January	=Sheet1!$B$5:$B$8						
15	March	=Sheet1!$D$5:$D$8						
16								

Qtr 1 / Qtr 2 / Invoice / Balance / Log / Sheet6 / Sheet

Ready   Sum=0   NUM

Start   Microsoft Excel - Bud...   9:23 AM

"Why would I do this?"

Typically, Excel inserts automatic page breaks
for you in your worksheet as needed to fit on
the printed page. However, you may not like
the placement of automatic page breaks, so you
may want to control where each new page
begins. You can set a manual page break
anywhere on the worksheet. Setting a manual
page break overrides the automatic page break
entered by Excel.

1 Click **A12**, which is one cell below where you want to insert a page break. Excel will print everything above row 12 on one page, and row 12 and everything below it on the next page.

> **NOTE** ▼
>
> You won't be able to perform this task unless a printer is installed. If no printer is installed, refer to your Windows manual.

2 Click **Insert** in the menu bar; then click **Page Break**. The manual page break appears above the active cell.

> **NOTE** ▼
>
> To insert a manual page break both above and to the left of the selected cell, click a cell that is not in the far left column of the worksheet.

3 Make sure the active cell is immediately below and to the right of the page break line(s). Click **Insert** in the menu bar. Then click **Remove Page Break**. The manual page break disappears above the active cell. ■

> **NOTE** ▼
>
> On-screen, manual page breaks have longer, thicker dashed lines than automatic page breaks.

Selecting a Print Area

"Why would I do this?"

Often, you will want to print specific portions
of a worksheet, such as a range of cells. You can
single out an area as a separate page and then
print that page. Excel will print only the
established print area. If the area is too large
to fit onto one page, Excel will break it into
multiple pages.

1 Let's select a print area that includes the range B5:E9. Click **File** in the menu bar, and then click **Page Setup**. Excel displays the Page options in the Page Setup dialog box. Click the **Sheet** tab to display the Sheet options. Notice the Print Area text box at the top of the dialog box.

NOTE ▼

You won't be able to perform this task unless a printer is installed. If no printer is installed, refer to your Windows manual.

2 Click in the **Print Area** text box to display the insertion point. Then type **B5:E9**. This step specifies the range B5:E9 as the print area.

NOTE ▼

Do not include the title, subtitle, and column and row headings in the print area. If you do, Excel will print the labels twice. In the next task, we will use these labels to print the column and row headings on every page.

3 Click **OK**. This step confirms your choice. Automatic page breaks appear surrounding the range B5:E9. ■

WHY WORRY?

To remove the print area, delete the cell coordinates in the Print Area text box. Excel does not have an Undo command to remove the print area.

Printing Column and Row Headings

"Why would I do this?"

Excel provides a way for you to select labels that are located on the top edge and left side of your worksheet, and print them on every page of the printout. This option is useful when a worksheet is too wide to print on a single page. Unless you use this option, the extra columns and rows will be printed on subsequent pages without any labels.

1 Click **File** in the menu bar. Then, click **Page Setup**. Excel displays the Page Setup dialog box; select the **Sheet** tab if it isn't already selected.

> **NOTE** ▼
>
> You won't be able to perform this task unless a printer is installed. If no printer is installed, refer to your Windows manual.

2 Click in the **Rows to Repeat at Top** text box. Then click anywhere in row 4. Excel displays **$4:$4** in the text box and a dashed line around the row in the worksheet.

> **WHY WORRY?**
>
> If you can't see row 4 because of the Page Setup dialog box, move the dialog box out of the way by dragging its title bar.

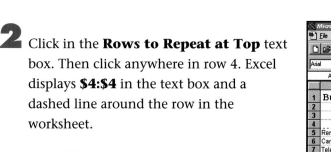

3 Click in the **Columns to Repeat at Left** text box. Then click anywhere in Column A. Excel displays **$A:$A** in the text box and a dashed line around the column in the worksheet. Click **OK**. ■

> **WHY WORRY?**
>
> To remove the repeated rows and columns, delete the cell coordinates in the Rows to Repeat at Top and Columns to Repeat at Left text boxes.

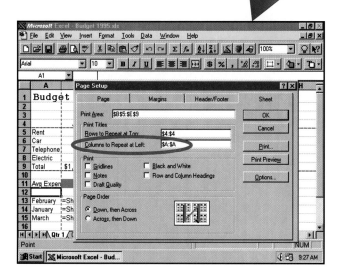

TASK 52

Adding Headers and Footers

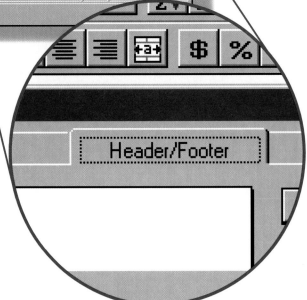

"Why would I do this?"

Headers and footers are lines of text that you can print on every page in a print job—headers at the top, footers at the bottom. You can include any text, the current date and time, the file name, and even format the information. Headers and footers typically help the reader identify things like "What report am I reading?" or "What page am I on?"

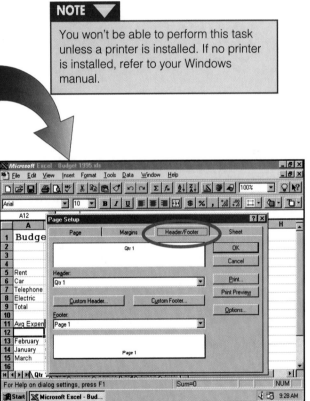

1 Let's create a header that contains the file name and a footer that will number the pages in our budget worksheet. Click **File** in the menu bar. Then click **Page Setup** to display the Page Setup dialog box.

NOTE

You won't be able to perform this task unless a printer is installed. If no printer is installed, refer to your Windows manual.

2 Click the **Header/Footer** tab to display the Header/Footer options. Notice the header and footer options in the box. Excel uses the name of the sheet, **Qtr 1**, as the header.

3 Click the down arrow next to the Header text box. A list of suggested header information displays. Scroll through the list until you see **Budget 1995.xls**; click it. The sample header appears at the top of the box. Notice that **Budget 1995.xls** is centered.

4 Also notice that the footer **Page 1** appears in the footer sample. Click the down arrow next to the Footer text box. A list of suggested footer information displays. Scroll through the list until you see **Page 1 of ?**; click it. The sample footer appears centered at the bottom of the box.

5 Click **OK** to close the Page Setup dialog box. On-screen, you cannot see the header and footer. To see them, you must preview the worksheet, which you will learn how to do in the next task. ■

NOTE ▼

You can include special codes in the header or footer. Excel also provides several header and footer formatting options. Refer to your Microsoft Excel documentation for a complete list of codes and formatting options.

WHY WORRY?

If something unexpected prints at the top or bottom of your worksheet, check the Header or Footer text box. If you don't want a header or footer, choose None in the Header or Footer suggestions list.

Previewing the Print Job

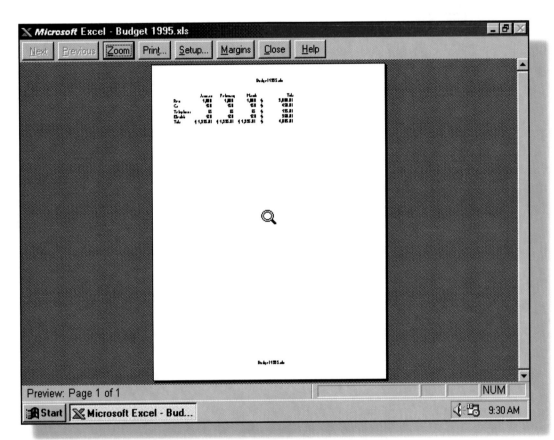

"Why would I do this?"

The Print Preview command lets you see worksheet pages on-screen as they will appear printed on paper, including page numbers, headers, footers, fonts, fonts sizes and styles, orientation, and margins. Previewing your worksheet is a great way to catch formatting errors such as incorrect margins, overlapped data, boldfaced data, and other text enhancements. You will save costly printer paper and time by first previewing your worksheet.

1 Click the **Print Preview** button on the Standard toolbar (the button with the piece of paper and a magnifying glass). You see a preview of how your worksheet will look when you print it.

> **NOTE** ▼
>
> To preview the worksheet, you must have a printer installed and your monitor must have graphics capability. If you see an error message, either you don't have a printer installed or your monitor probably cannot display the worksheet. Install a printer and print the worksheet to see how it looks.

2 Click the **Zoom** button at the top of the screen to enlarge the preview to its actual size. By zooming the worksheet to actual size, you can examine the printout more closely. Click **Zoom** again to return to the original Print Preview size. To exit the Preview, click the **Close** button. Excel redisplays the worksheet. ■

> **NOTE** ▼
>
> You can also zoom by clicking anywhere on the Print Preview page. Notice, in the previous figure, that the mouse pointer changes to look like a magnifying glass as you move it over the page.

> **WHY WORRY?**
>
> You can also press the **Esc** key to quit the preview.

Printing the Worksheet

"Why would I do this?"

Excel gives you many print options for customizing the way you print your worksheets. You can change the orientation, margins, or reduce or enlarge the printout to fit on an 8 1/2-by-11-inch sheet of paper. Refer to your Microsoft Excel documentation for complete information on the options in the Page Setup dialog box.

179

1 Let's print the budget worksheet. Click **File** in the menu bar. Then click **Page Setup**. Excel displays the Page Setup dialog box. Click the **Page** tab to display the Page options.

NOTE ▼

You won't be able to perform this task unless a printer is installed. If no printer is installed, refer to your Windows manual.

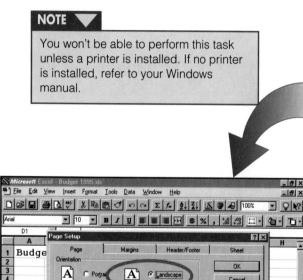

2 Click the **Landscape** option button to select the Landscape orientation and tell Excel to print the worksheet sideways.

NOTE ▼

If you don't need to set any special printing options, you can print the worksheet by clicking the **Print** button in the Standard toolbar. It's the fourth button from the left edge of the toolbar.

3 Click the **Margins** tab to display the Margins options. Excel uses the following default margin settings: Left .75", Right .75", Top 1", and Bottom 1". Double-click in the **Top** text box and type **2**. This step resets the new top margin to two inches.

NOTE ▼

You can see the new top margin in the Preview sample in the middle of the box.

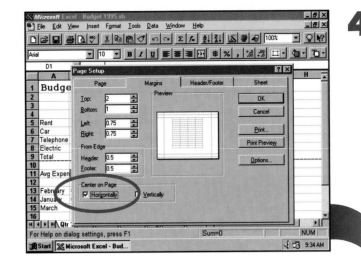

4 Click the **Center on Page Horizontally** check box. Excel will center the page between the left and right margins based on the current left and right margin settings. Now let's print the worksheet.

NOTE ▼

You can see that the worksheet is centered horizontally in the Preview sample in the middle of the box.

5 Click the **Print** button. Excel displays the Print dialog box. You see the name of your printer at the top of the dialog box. Click **OK** to start the print job. ■

WHY WORRY?

To reset any options in the Page Setup dialog box, follow the same procedure. You cannot use an Undo command to reverse the settings. During a print job, Excel displays a dialog box on-screen. To stop the print job, click **Cancel**.

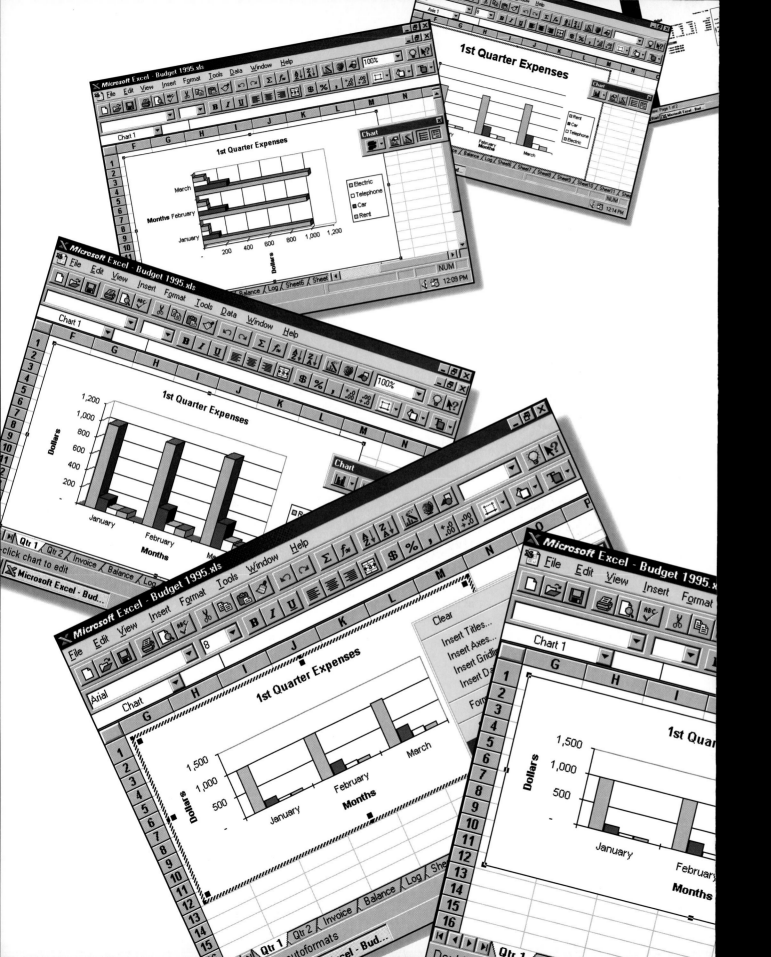

PART VII

Working with Charts and Maps

Worksheet information can be both useful and impressive in presentations. You can print just the worksheet if you only need numerical detail, or you can create a chart from the data in the worksheet. Charts are great for visually depicting and increasing the understanding of relationships between numerical values; at the same time, charts greatly enhance a presentation.

Before you create a chart, you should familiarize yourself with the elements of a chart. With the exception of pie charts, all charts contain at least two axes—one vertical axis and a horizontal axis (pie charts contain no axes, and some charts contain more than one vertical or horizontal axis). The *Y axis* is the vertical axis; Excel refers to this axis as the *value axis*. It displays the values of the information you plot. The *X axis* is the horizontal axis; Excel refers to this axis as the *category axis,* because it contains divisions or classifications of information (categories) about your data. We'll talk more about categories in a moment.

A chart plots values from worksheet cells—think of these as data points. Data points are grouped into bars, pie slices, lines, or other elements on a chart—we refer to these grouped data points as *data series*. For example, a column chart would contain bars that depict a series of values for the same item—for example, monthly sales figures or monthly staffing levels. You'll see labels describing each data series in the legend of the chart.

Categories show the number of elements in a data series. You might use two data series to compare the sales of two different offices, and four categories to compare these sales over four quarters. On a chart like this one, sales dollars would appear on the value axis (the vertical or Y axis), each office's name would appear in the legend of the chart, and Quarter 1, Quarter 2, Quarter 3, and Quarter 4 would appear as categories on the category axis (the horizontal or X axis). Categories usually correspond to the number of columns that you have selected in your worksheet. *Category labels* describe the categories below the horizontal axis. These labels come from the column headings of the data you include in the chart.

The *chart text* includes all the labels on the chart. Most chart text has to be added to the basic chart. You can also format labels by changing the fonts, font sizes, font styles, and colors. Text is useful for explaining various elements on the chart. Excel automatically assigns values to the value axis when you create a chart, but you can override the default settings and set the minimum and maximum values. You can also add a text label to the value axis to describe what the values represent.

The *plot area* consists of the actual bars, lines, or other elements that represent the data series. Everything outside the plot area helps explain what is inside the plot area. You can format the plot area by changing the patterns and colors of the data series. A *legend* contains the labels for the data series in the chart and serves as a "key" to the chart. To create the legend, Excel uses labels in the first column of the chart range. The legend will appear at the right of the chart data. However, you can move the legend anywhere you want on the chart. *Gridlines* are dotted lines you can add to a chart so that you can read the plotted data more easily. You can create three types of gridlines: horizontal, vertical, and a combination of both. After you add the gridlines, you can change their colors and patterns.

In this part, you learn how to create a chart quickly and easily with the ChartWizard, which leads you, like the other *Wizards* in Excel, step-by-step through an otherwise complex procedure. The ChartWizard guides you through the process, providing help every step of the way. While using the ChartWizard, you can preview the sample chart before you finish creating the chart and make changes. You'll also learn how to use Excel's Chart AutoFormat feature, which applies one of several predefined formats to your chart, making formatting faster and easier because you don't need to apply formatting to each individual chart element. In subsequent tasks in this part, you learn how to modify the individual components of the chart.

Mapping is a new feature in Excel for Windows 95. With this feature, you can use your data to create a map and analyze the geographic impact of your data. With this feature, you can easily show, for example, sales data for a particular region. One column of your data contains some kind of geographic information, such as state names or countries. In the last few tasks in this part, we'll introduce you to mapping in Excel.

Creating a Chart

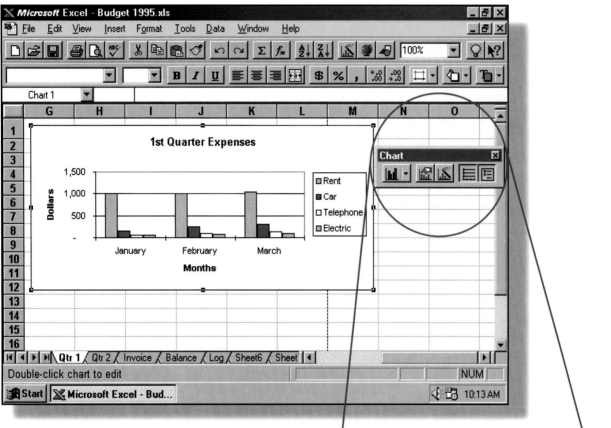

"Why would I do this?"

You create charts in Excel using the Chart-Wizard. The ChartWizard leads you step-by-step through the tasks for creating a chart. Excel plots the data and creates the chart where you specify on the worksheet. We'll continue working with the Budget 1995 worksheet that we used in Part VI.

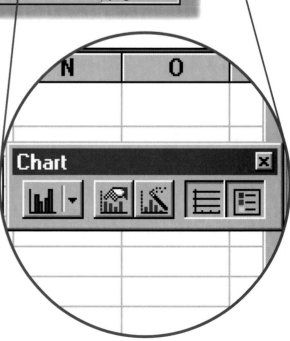

1 Let's start by clearing the print area. Choose **File**, **Print Area**, then **Clear Print Area**. The page breaks disappear from the worksheet. Now change the data in the worksheet so that your computer screen matches the figure.

WHY WORRY?

To remove the box surrounding the numbers in Column E, click the list button on the right side of the Borders button list, and then click in the upper left corner of the box.

2 Select cells **A4** to **D8** to select the range you want to chart. (Before you can create a chart, you must select data in the worksheet.)

NOTE ▼

If Excel doesn't display the chart toolbar, choose the **View**, **Toolbars** command, click the **Chart** check box, and then click **OK**.

3 Click the **ChartWizard** button on the Standard toolbar. A marquee surrounds the selected data. The mouse pointer changes to a cross-hair pointer with a tiny column chart attached. The ChartWizard cross-hair pointer lets you create a box to specify the size and shape of the chart on the worksheet.

4 Click cell **G1** and drag the cross-hair pointer to cell **M12**; then release the mouse button. Cell G1 is where you want the upper left corner of the chart to appear. Cell M12 is where you want the lower right corner of the chart to appear. Excel displays a solid-line rectangle while you drag to specify the size and shape of the chart on the worksheet. Releasing the mouse button brings up the ChartWizard - Step 1 of 5 dialog box and the Chart toolbar.

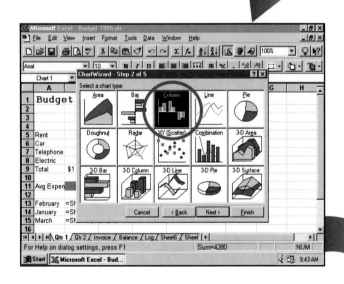

5 Click the **Next** button to confirm the selected range—in this case, **A4:D8**. From the ChartWizard - Step 2 of 5 dialog box, you choose a chart type. The **column chart** is the default chart type.

NOTE ▼

The type of chart you should select depends on what you're trying to emphasize. A column chart tends to emphasize variations over time while a bar chart tends to emphasize information at a specific point in time.

6 Click the **Next** button to confirm the type of chart—in this case, the column chart. From the ChartWizard - Step 3 of 5 dialog box, you specify the format you want for your chart. Column chart 6 is the default format for the column chart type—a column chart with horizontal gridlines. This is the format we want.

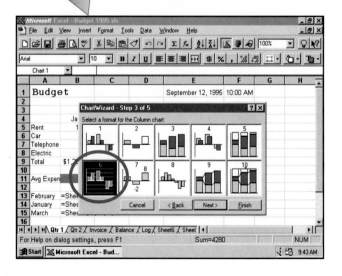

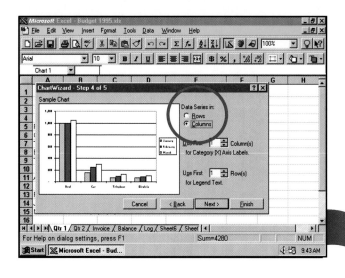

7 Click the **Next** button to confirm the format for the chart type—in this case, Column chart 6. Excel displays the Chart-Wizard - Step 4 of 5 dialog box, which contains a sample chart. Initially, the data series is charted in columns. As you can see, each bar represents a month, and you see three bars for each expense in the budget. We want Excel to chart the data series in rows—in this case, each bar will represent an expense in the budget, and you'll see four bars for each month in the chart.

8 Click the **Rows** option button to show the data series in rows. Excel redisplays the chart with January, February, and March as the category (X) axis labels. The expense names appear in the legend for the data series. By default, Excel labels the category axis and the value axis using at least one row and one column in the range you selected when you started creating this chart. The other two choices in this dialog box let you specify the additional rows and columns you want to appear as labels.

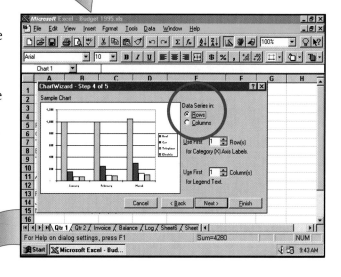

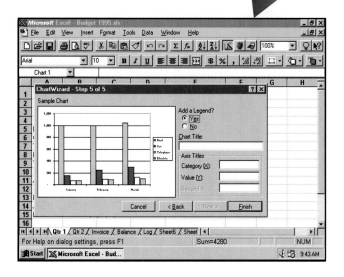

9 Click the **Next** button, which confirms the options for the data series and first column and first row. Excel displays the final dialog box, ChartWizard - Step 5 of 5, with the sample chart again and gives you options for adding a legend and titles. Let's keep the legend that explains the data series and add a chart title and axes titles.

10 Click in the **Chart Title** text box or press the **Tab** key. Then type **1st Quarter-Expenses**. Excel redisplays the chart in the sample box with the title at the top. Add titles for each axis: call the **Category (X)** axis **Months** and call the **Value (Y)** axis **Dollars**.

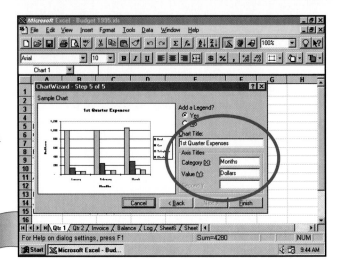

11 Click the **Finish** button to add the new chart to the worksheet at the specified location. Scroll to the right to see the entire chart—you'll also see the Chart toolbar. Click the **Save** button on the Standard toolbar to save the file. ■

WHY WORRY?

You can stop the process of creating a chart with the ChartWizard at any time. Just click the **Cancel** button in the ChartWizard dialog box; then start over. If you want to return to the previous ChartWizard dialog box, click the **Back** button.

Using Chart AutoFormat

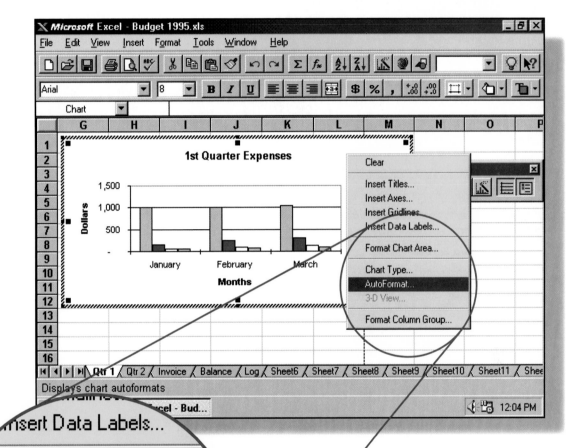

"Why would I do this?"

Using the Chart AutoFormat feature, you can simultaneously apply a set of predefined chart types and formats to a selected chart on the worksheet. In fact, the Chart AutoFormat feature provides the only way to change the format of a chart after you create it.

1 The chart is currently selected—you can tell by the small black squares called selection handles that surround it. Double-click anywhere in the chart area. Excel displays the chart in its own window, and the thin black line that previously surrounded the chart changes to a broken line.

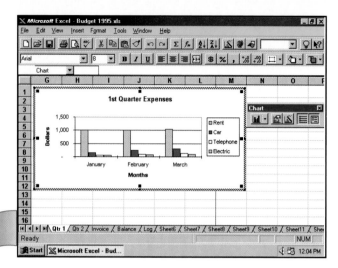

2 In the chart area, click the *right* mouse button. Excel displays a shortcut menu of commands you can use to modify the appearance of the chart.

3 Choose the **AutoFormat** command. Excel displays the AutoFormat dialog box. A list of chart types and a palette of corresponding chart formats appear in the box. The Column chart **6** format is currently selected.

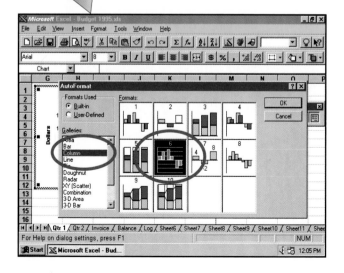

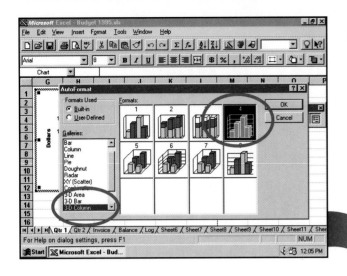

4 From the **Galleries** list box, choose **3-D Column**. Column chart **4** format is currently selected, and we'll use that format.

5 Click **OK**. This step confirms your choice. Excel changes the chart to the new format. You may notice that the months don't fit on the Category axis anymore—we'll fix that in the next task. Click the **Save** button on the Standard toolbar to save the file. ■

WHY WORRY?

To remove the format, click the **Undo** button on the Standard toolbar before you save the chart. Then repeat the previous steps and choose a different chart type and/or format.

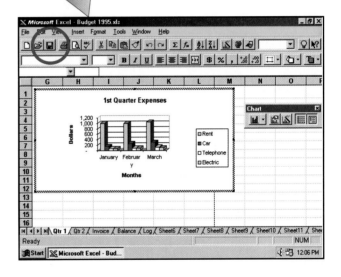

Changing the Chart's Size and Shape

"Why would I do this?"

When you first create the chart, the outline you drag for the chart determines the size and shape of the chart in the worksheet. After you create the chart, you can change the size of the chart or even move it to a different location in the worksheet.

1 Click cell **F1** and press **Del** to delete the time in cell F1 to make room for widening the chart. Click anywhere on the chart to reselect the chart. Excel displays selection handles on the chart's border and the Chart toolbar reappears. You use selection handles to resize a chart.

NOTE ▼
When you click in the worksheet, the Chart toolbar disappears because the chart is no longer selected.

2 Move the mouse pointer to the left middle selection handle and when the cursor becomes a double-headed arrow, drag the chart to the left, aligning the chart with the left edge of column F. This step makes the chart wider.

NOTE ▼
Notice that the months now fit along the X axis.

3 Move the mouse pointer to the bottom middle selection handle, and when the cursor changes to a double-headed arrow, drag the chart down to the bottom edge of row **16**. This step makes the chart taller. ■

WHY WORRY?
If you don't like the size and shape of the chart, drag the selection handles in the direction you want until you get the desired results.

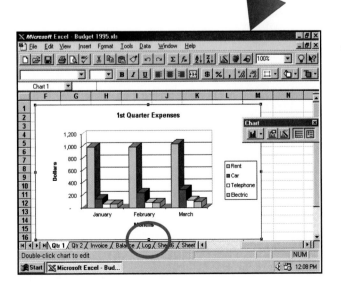

Changing the Chart Type

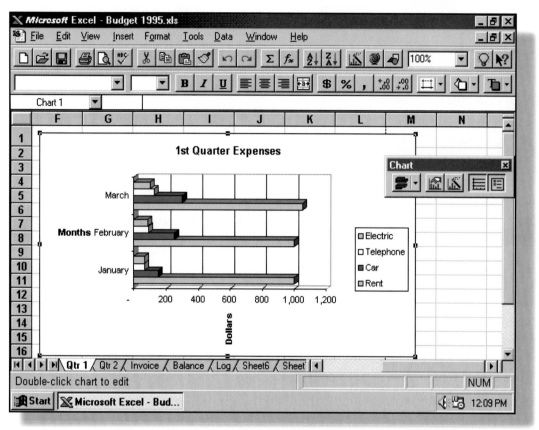

"Why would I do this?"

You can take an existing chart and turn it into a different chart instantly at any time. You will find that certain chart types are best for certain situations. It might be more dramatic, appropriate, or meaningful to display the data in a different type of chart. For example, you can usually spot trends more easily with a line chart, while a pie chart is best for showing parts of a whole. A line chart shows trends over time.

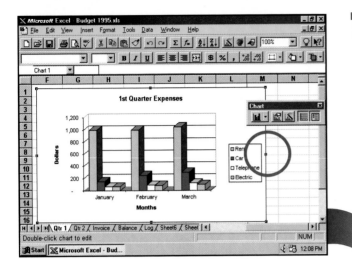

1 Click anywhere on the chart. Excel places handles around the chart, and the Chart toolbar appears.

NOTE ▼

If Excel doesn't display the Chart toolbar, choose the **View**, **Toolbars** command, click the check box next to **Chart**, and then click **OK**.

2 Click the down arrow next to the **Chart Type** button on the Chart toolbar. Excel displays the palette of predesigned charts.

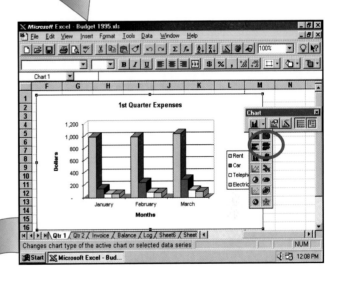

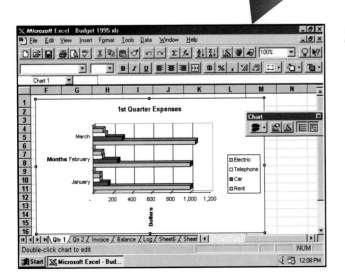

3 In the second column, click the second chart from the top. Excel changes the chart to the horizontal column format, showing 3-D horizontal bars. This looks like a good representation for your data; but let's try switching to the line chart.

4 Click the down arrow next to the **Chart Type** button. In the first column, click the fourth chart from the top to select a chart type—in this case, the line chart. Excel changes the chart to reflect your choice. Notice that the lines represent the expenses by month. It is easier to depict trends in the column charts than in the line chart. So, let's see what the pie chart looks like.

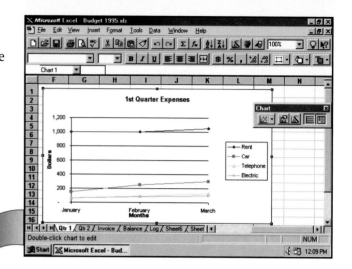

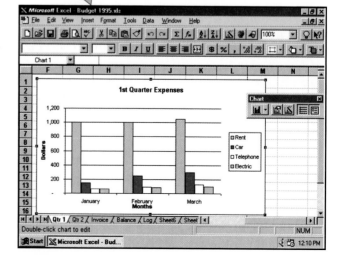

5 Click the down arrow next to the **Chart Type** button. In the first column, click the fifth chart from the top. Excel changes the chart to a pie chart format, which shows that each month makes up one-third of the data represented in the chart. Since the pie chart doesn't depict the data as well as the column chart, let's switch back to the horizontal column chart type.

6 Click the down arrow next to the **Chart Type** button. In the first column, click the third chart from the top. Excel changes the chart to the vertical column format. ■

Formatting the Title

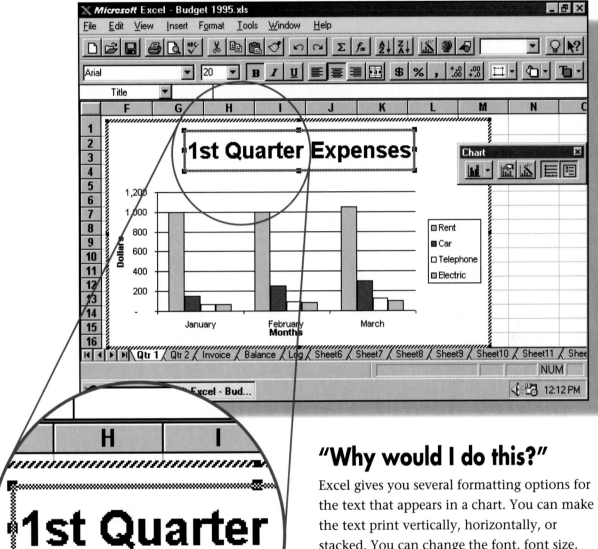

"Why would I do this?"

Excel gives you several formatting options for the text that appears in a chart. You can make the text print vertically, horizontally, or stacked. You can change the font, font size, style, and color of any text. You can also move text anywhere you want on the chart. You might want to change the font for the title to a larger font and boldface the title to draw attention to it.

1 Let's make the chart title larger. Double-click the chart to display it in its own window. Then, click the **title** at the top of the chart. A border with selection handles surrounds the title.

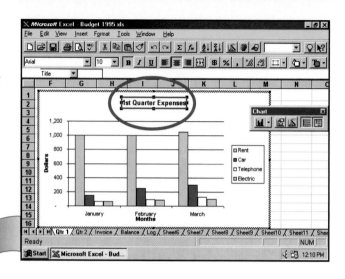

2 Click the down arrow next to the **Font Size** box on the Formatting toolbar. Excel displays a list of font sizes. Click a larger number; then press **Esc** to deselect the title. In the figure, the new font size is **20**. ∎

NOTE ▼

The font sizes may vary, depending on the type of printer you have and the fonts installed.

TASK 60
Changing Axis Scales

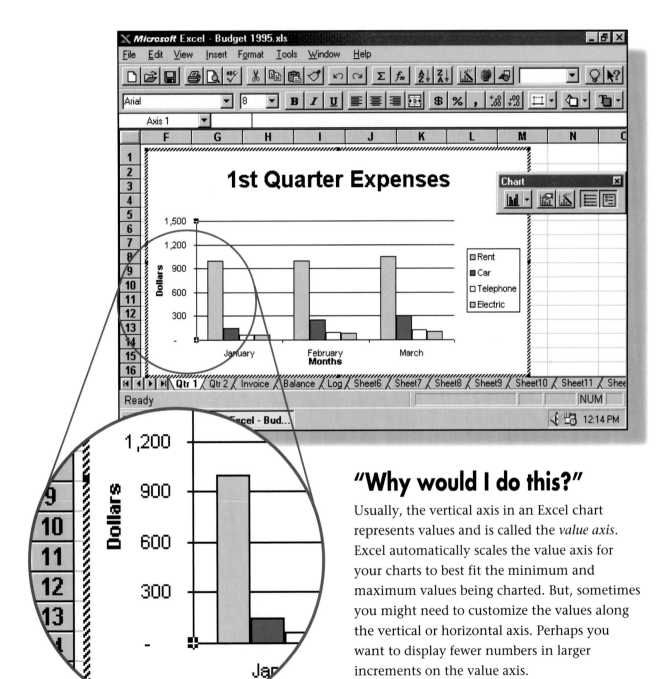

"Why would I do this?"

Usually, the vertical axis in an Excel chart represents values and is called the *value axis*. Excel automatically scales the value axis for your charts to best fit the minimum and maximum values being charted. But, sometimes you might need to customize the values along the vertical or horizontal axis. Perhaps you want to display fewer numbers in larger increments on the value axis.

201

1 Click the **vertical axis** (Y-axis) line to select the value axis. Selection boxes (small black squares) appear at each end of the value axis.

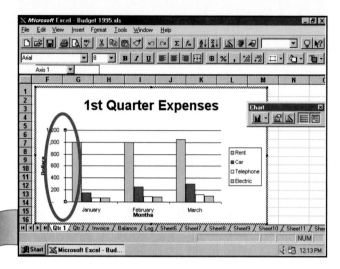

2 Double-click the **vertical axis** line. Excel displays the Format Axis dialog box. Click the **Scale** tab to display the Scale options.

NOTE ▼

The Format Axis dialog box contains various options for changing the axes. For more information on these options, refer to your Microsoft Excel documentation.

3 Double-click in the **Maximum** text box and type **1500**. This step enters the high value on the value axis—in this case, 1500.

NOTE ▼

When you change any of the preset values, Excel automatically clears the Auto check box.

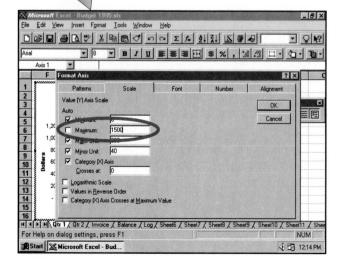

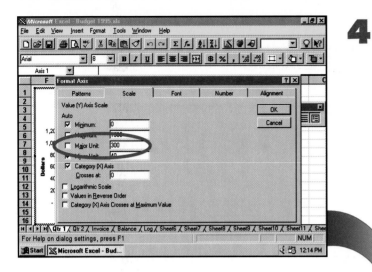

4 Double-click in the **Major Unit** text box and type **300** to change the interval between values on the value axis—in this case, 300. Again, Excel clears the Auto check box.

5 Click **OK** to accept your changes. As you can see, the highest value at the top of the vertical axis is **1500** and the interval between values is **300**. ∎

WHY WORRY?

If you don't get the scale numbers you want, just click the **Undo** button on the Standard toolbar. If you want to clear the settings and return to the original default values, reopen the Format Axis dialog box and select the appropriate Auto check boxes.

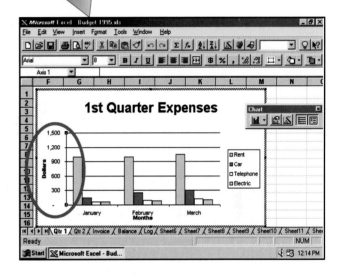

Formatting the Axes

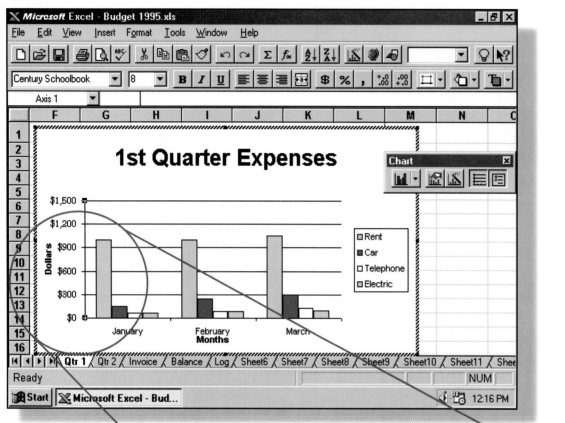

"Why would I do this?"

You can change the look of the scale indicators on the axes. For example, you can change the style, color, and weight of the axis line. You can change the format of the numbers that appear on an axis scale by adding dollar signs, decimal points, commas, and percent signs.

In this task, you'll add dollar signs to the values on the vertical axis in your column chart. Then you'll change the font for the values on the vertical axis.

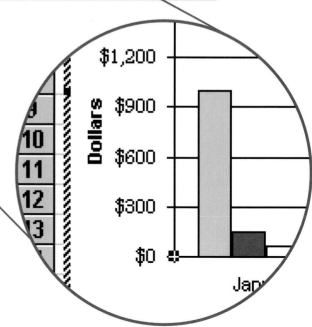

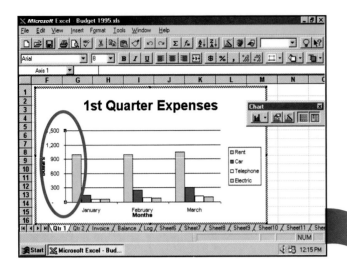

1 Click the **vertical axis** line, if necessary, to select the value axis. Selection boxes (small black squares) appear at each end of the value axis.

2 Double-click the **vertical axis** line. Excel displays the Format Axis dialog box. Click the **Number** tab to display the Number options.

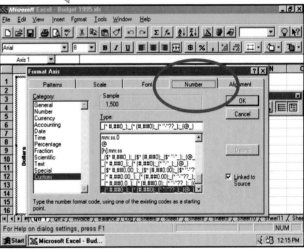

> **NOTE** ▼
>
> You can change the Patterns, Scale, Font, Number, and Alignment options in the dialog box. See your Microsoft Excel documentation for complete information.

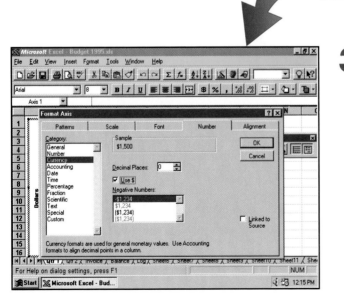

3 Choose **Currency** from the Category list. If necessary, click the **Use $** check box to place a check in it. The sample **$1,500.00** appears at the top of the dialog box. Use the spinner box to change the **Decimal Places** to **0**.

4 To change the font on the vertical axis, you need the vertical axis selected and the Format Axis dialog box open. Since these two conditions are already true (see Steps 1 and 2), click the **Font** tab to display the Font options. Then click any font in the list. In the figure next to this step, the new font is **Century Schoolbook**.

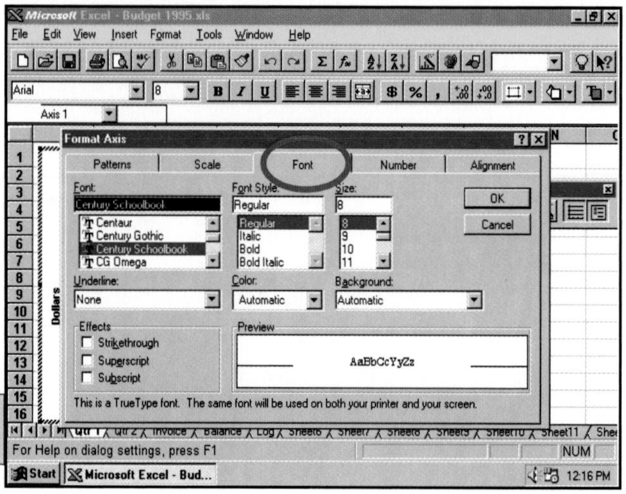

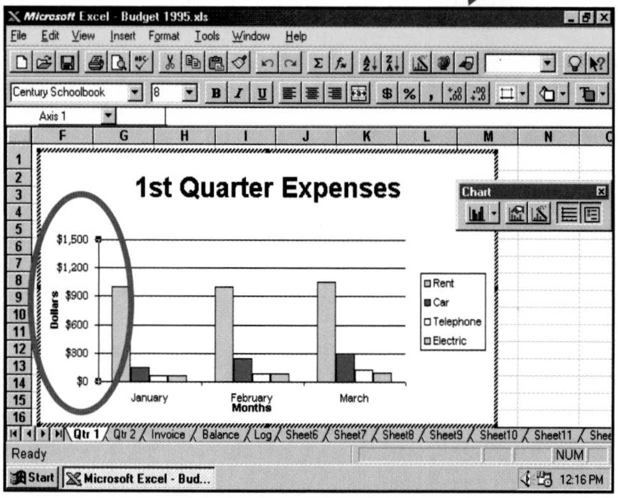

5 Click **OK** to confirm your choice. Excel adds dollar signs to the values on the vertical axis scale and changes the font for the values on the vertical axis scale. ■

TASK 62
Changing the Patterns of Data Series

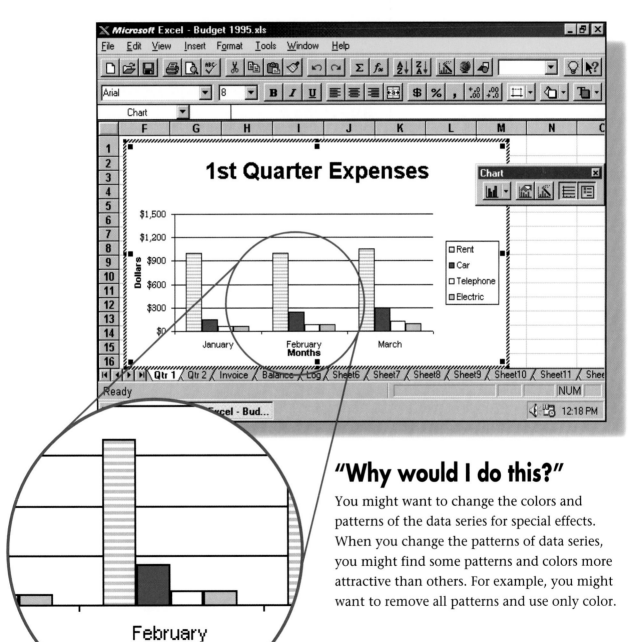

"Why would I do this?"

You might want to change the colors and patterns of the data series for special effects. When you change the patterns of data series, you might find some patterns and colors more attractive than others. For example, you might want to remove all patterns and use only color.

1 Make sure that the chart is selected and appears in its own window. Then, click the first data series (the bar that represents the rent for January) to select all the bars that represent rent. Small squares appear in each of the bars. These squares are called *selection boxes*.

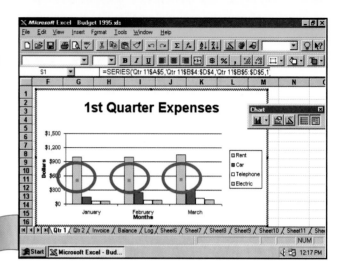

2 Double-click any selected bar to display the **Patterns** tab in the Format Data Series dialog box.

> **NOTE** ▼
>
> This tab is divided into two parts. The Border options on the Patterns tab affect the perimeter of the selected element, including the style, color, and weight of the border line. The Area options control the inside of the element, such as its pattern and color.

3 From the **Area** options, click the down arrow next to the **Pattern** text box. Excel displays a palette of patterns and colors. In the first column of the palette, click the second pattern from the top. This step selects the horizontal striped pattern.

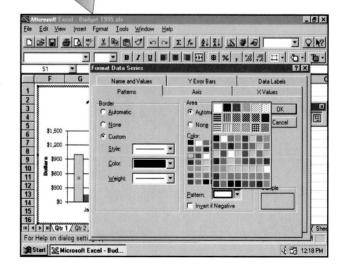

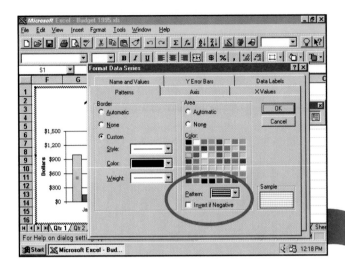

4 The sample appears in the lower right corner of the dialog box.

5 Click **OK**. Then press **Esc** to deselect the data series. This step confirms your choice. Excel displays the bars in the horizontal striped pattern with the default color—in this case, blue. Notice that the legend contains the new pattern for Rent. ■

WHY WORRY?

To remove the pattern from a data series, click the **Undo** button on the Standard toolbar. Then repeat the previous steps and choose a different pattern or a color.

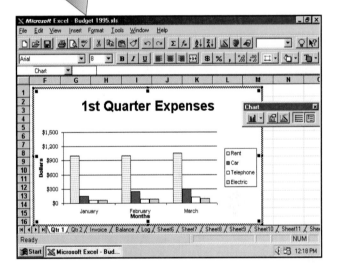

Changing the Category Labels

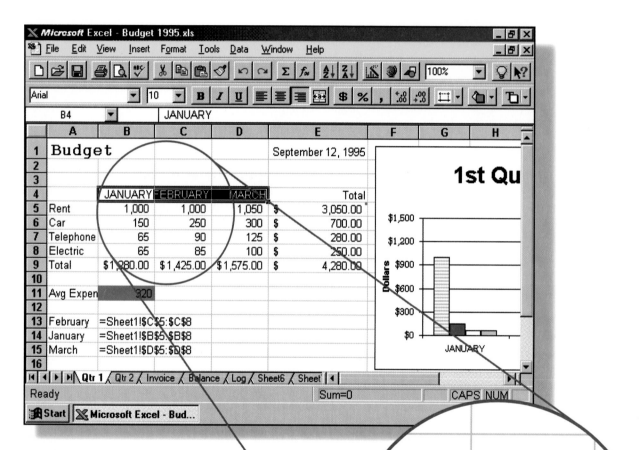

"Why would I do this?"

Excel places category labels next to the horizontal axis along the bottom of the chart. If you don't want the category labels that go with your chart, you can change them. For instance, you might want to abbreviate long category labels that run into each other. That way, all the labels will fit properly on the category (X) axis.

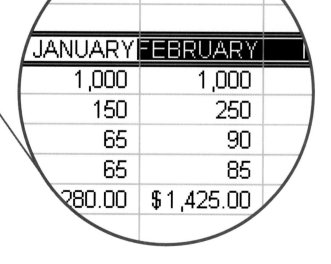

1 Click any cell in the worksheet twice to deselect the chart. Then press **Ctrl+Home** to return to cell **A1**. Now you can see the worksheet. Select cells **B4** to **D4** to select the range where we will enter the category labels we want in the chart.

WHY WORRY?

You'll know the chart is no longer selected when no black handles appear around it and the Chart toolbar disappears.

2 Retype the names of the months in capital letters. Press **Enter** after typing **JANUARY** in cell **B4**—Excel moves automatically to **C4** and waits for you to type **FEBRUARY**. Then scroll to the right so that you can see the chart. As you type, Excel instantly updates the chart to reflect the changes in the worksheet. The new category labels appear at the bottom of the chart. ■

NOTE ▼

The same principal holds true for data. If you change any of the numbers in the cells included in the chart range, Excel will automatically update the chart to reflect the new values.

WHY WORRY?

The data in the cells may overlap when they are filled with capital letters—no problem. Excel doesn't care and will display them properly on the chart.

Adding Text Labels

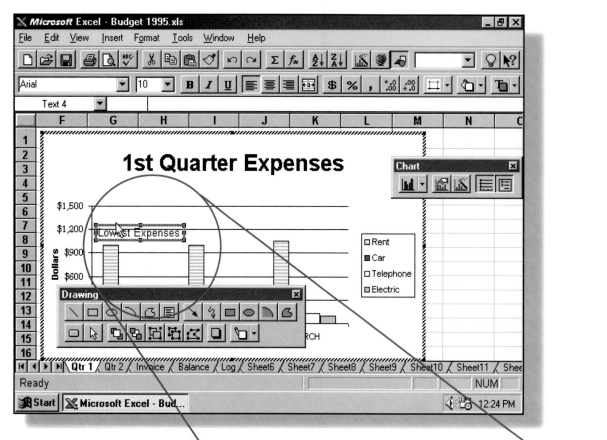

"Why would I do this?"

Adding text labels makes the chart's data more meaningful and may accentuate a certain bar, line, or slice of pie in the chart. You might want to add a text label to point out the highest or lowest value in the chart.

In this task, you'll continue to work with the chart from the previous task. You'll create a text label, **Lowest Expenses!**, and place it next to the January data series.

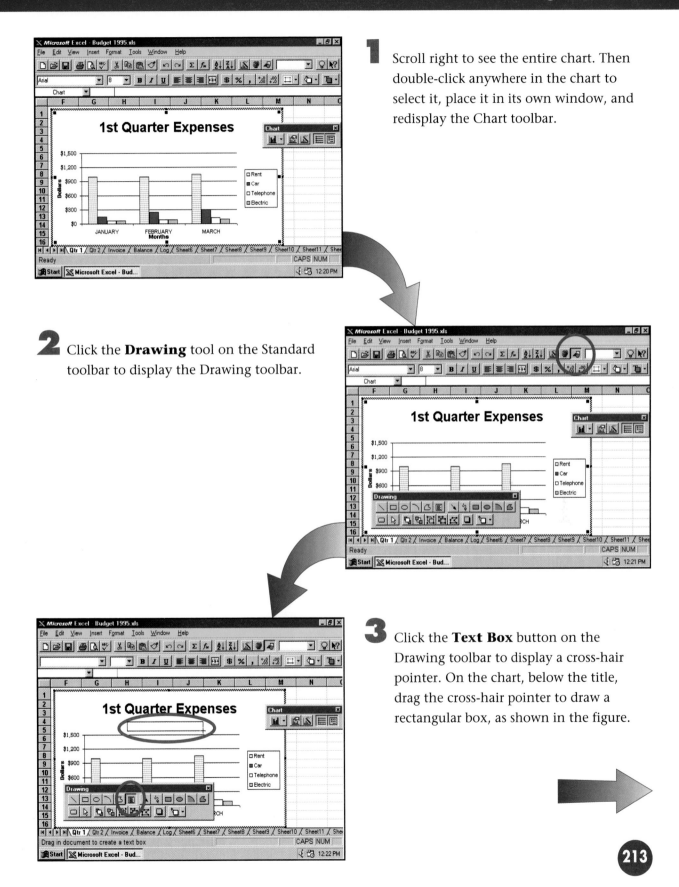

1 Scroll right to see the entire chart. Then double-click anywhere in the chart to select it, place it in its own window, and redisplay the Chart toolbar.

2 Click the **Drawing** tool on the Standard toolbar to display the Drawing toolbar.

3 Click the **Text Box** button on the Drawing toolbar to display a cross-hair pointer. On the chart, below the title, drag the cross-hair pointer to draw a rectangular box, as shown in the figure.

4 When you release the mouse button, Excel adds a text box to the chart.

NOTE ▼

If you don't see the outline or the insertion point, click where you think they should appear.

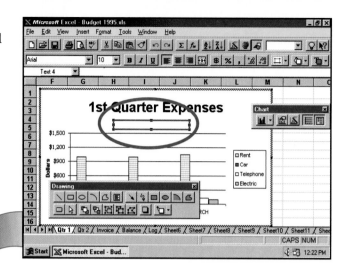

5 Type **Lowest Expenses** to enter the text for the label and click outside the text box to confirm that you are finished typing text. **Lowest Expenses** appears on the chart.

WHY WORRY?

You can close the Drawing toolbar at this point by clicking the **X** in the upper right corner of the toolbar.

6 Click **Lowest Expenses**. A border with selection handles surrounds the text. If necessary, use the selection handles to shrink the box so that it is the same size as the text. Then drag the text box above the data series for January. ■

WHY WORRY?

To remove the selection handles from the text box, press **Esc**. To remove a text label from the chart, click the text label to select it, and then press **Del**.

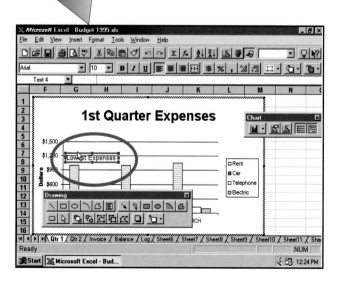

Printing a Chart

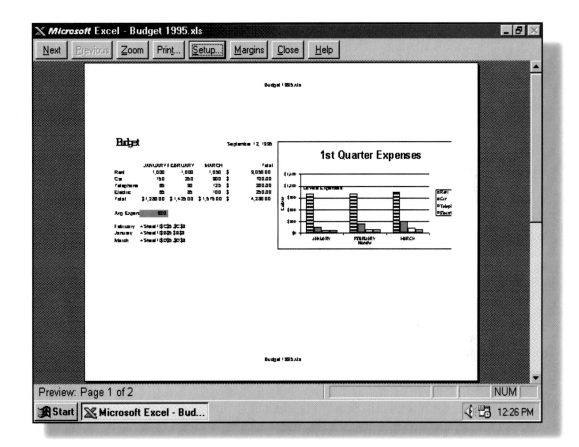

"Why would I do this?"

You can print the chart with its worksheet as you would any worksheet. You might want to print the chart and worksheet together for a presentation. That way, you can easily see trends in a series of values.

In this task, you'll print the worksheet and the chart you created in previous tasks.

1 Click any cell in the worksheet twice to deselect the chart. Choose **File**, **Print Area**, **Clear Print Area** to remove any automatic page breaks Excel may have inserted.

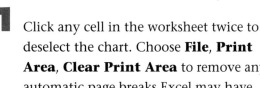

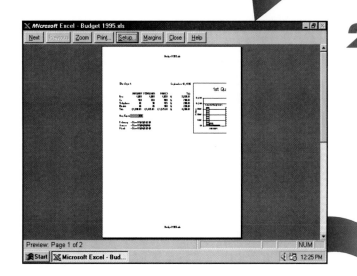

2 Click the **Print Preview** button on the Standard toolbar to display the worksheet on-screen as it will print. As you can see, both the worksheet and chart appear on-screen in the preview window, but you can see only a portion of the chart. Let's change the orientation to Landscape.

3 Click **Setup** to display the Page Setup dialog box and click the Page tab. Then, click the **Landscape** button in the Orientation box.

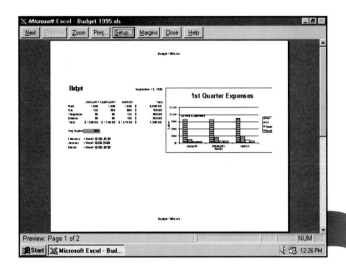

4 When you click **OK**, Excel closes the dialog box and redisplays the worksheet in landscape orientation, where you can see the worksheet data and the chart.

WHY WORRY?

If you still can't see the entire worksheet and chart, click the **Margins** button. Then, drag the left margin line to the left and the right margin line to the right. As you pass the mouse pointer over the margin boundaries, it changes shape to a two-headed arrow pointing left and right.

5 Click the **Print** button on the toolbar to display the Print dialog box. From the Page Range options, click the **Page(s)** option button, type **1** in the **From** box, press **Tab**, and type **1** in the **To** box. This step enters the range of pages to print—in this case, only page 1. Click **OK.** Excel prints the worksheet and the chart. ■

NOTE ▼

If you are printing a chart on a printer that doesn't print color, you must change the print chart options to print in black and white. Otherwise, you will not get the printout results you want. Select the **File**, **Page Setup** command; click the **Sheet** tab, and, in the Print box, select the **Black and White** option.

WHY WORRY?

If a portion of your page is cut off, you may have shortened the margins too much (laser printers require at least .5 inches around all edges of the page). Choose **File**, **Page Setup** and click the **Margins** tab. Make sure each margin is at least .5 inches.

Creating a Map

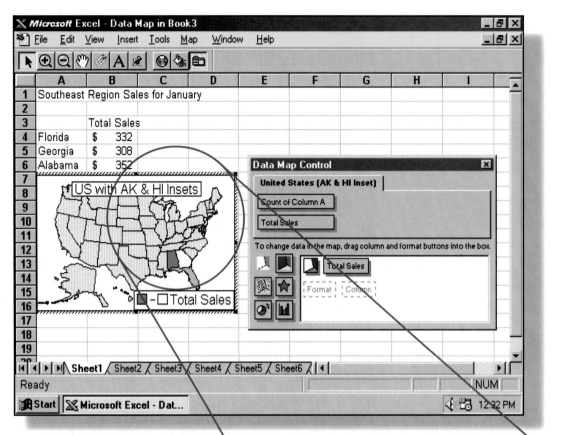

"Why would I do this?"

Whenever you work with data that is
geographic in nature, displaying the data on
a map is a most effective tool. Using Excel's
new Map feature, you can enter data into a
worksheet, and Excel will draw a map and
include your data.

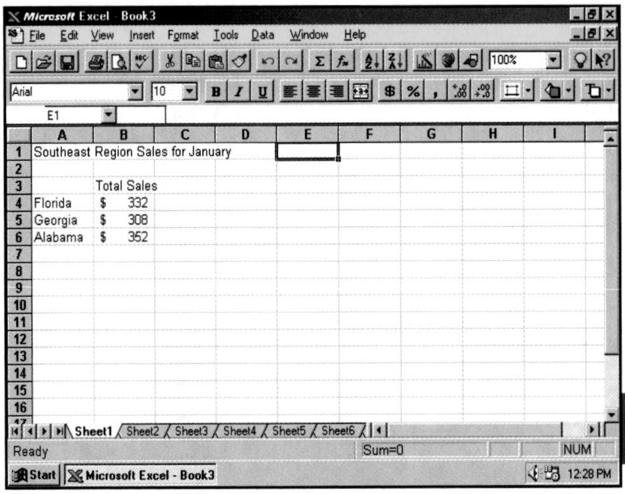

1 Start a new worksheet and set it up so that it looks like the one in the figure next to this step.

NOTE ▼

To create a map in Excel, you must include geographic information in one column of the worksheet.

2 Select **A3:B6**—the range containing the information you want to show on the map.

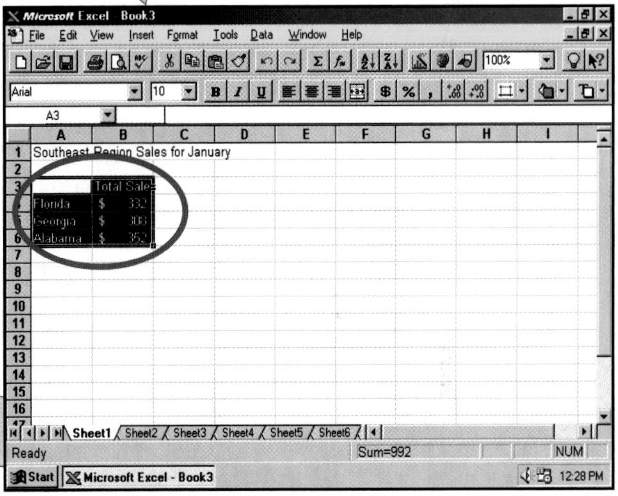

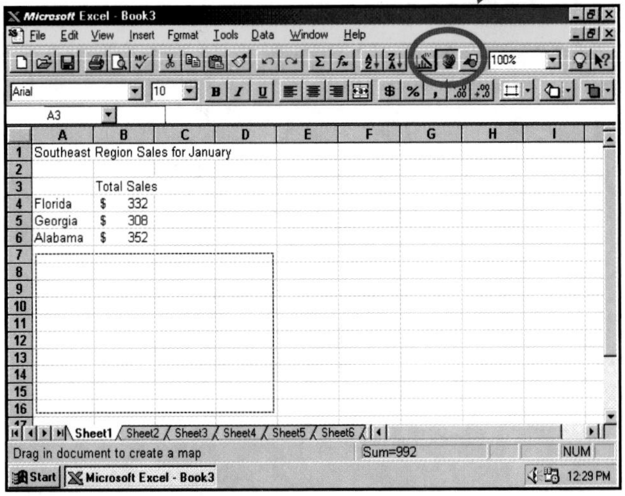

3 Click the **Map** tool on the Standard toolbar. The mouse pointer changes shapes to indicate you're about to draw a map. Starting in A7, drag across **A7:D16**, the location where you want to place the map. Excel draws an outline of the box that will contain the map while you drag.

4 When you release the mouse button, Excel displays either the Unable to Create Map dialog box or the Multiple Maps Available dialog box. In either case, choose the map on which you want Excel to base the map it draws. In our example, choose **United States including Alaska and Hawaii**.

WHY WORRY?

You may have to wait awhile for Excel to create your map. Don't worry; that's normal.

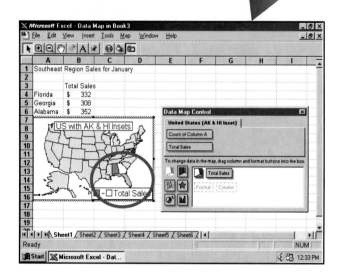

5 After you click **OK**, Excel displays a map and the Data Map Control dialog box. Notice that the three states in the worksheet data are highlighted in the map. Also, notice the new Map toolbar and menus on-screen. ■

Zooming In and Out

"Why would I do this?"

Sometimes, you want to focus on only a portion of the map Excel draws. Using the Zoom feature, you can "blow up" the portion of the map to which you're trying to draw attention. Start by closing the Data Map Control dialog box—click the X in the upper right corner of the box.

1 With the map selected and appearing in its own window, double-click the **Zoom In** tool on the Map toolbar. When you move the mouse pointer onto the map, the mouse pointer shape will change to a magnifying glass containing a plus sign.

NOTE ▼

The map is selected and in its own window when you see black selection handles and a cross-hatched outline around it. If the map isn't selected, double-click it.

2 Click over the area you want to enlarge. In our example, place the mouse so that the magnifying glass touches all three states, and then click. Make the map even larger by clicking a second time while the magnifying glass touches all three states. ■

WHY WORRY?

If you need to reopen the Data Map Control dialog box, click the last tool on the Map toolbar.

WHY WORRY?

If you zoom in "too close," click the **Zoom Out** tool and click the area of the map you zoomed in on.

Changing the Legend

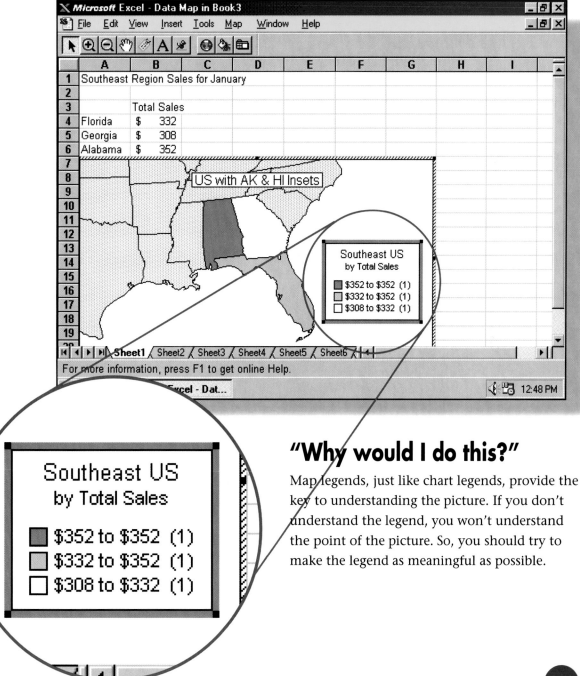

"Why would I do this?"

Map legends, just like chart legends, provide the key to understanding the picture. If you don't understand the legend, you won't understand the point of the picture. So, you should try to make the legend as meaningful as possible.

1 Click the **Pointer** tool to stop zooming. Then, click the legend in the map. Excel highlights the legend to indicate that you selected it.

2 Double-click the legend. Excel presents the Edit Legend dialog box.

3 Remove the check from the **Use Compact Format** check box by clicking the box. Change the title to **Southeast US**; the subtitle should remain **By Total Sales**. When you click **OK**, Excel presents a much more meaningful legend on your map.

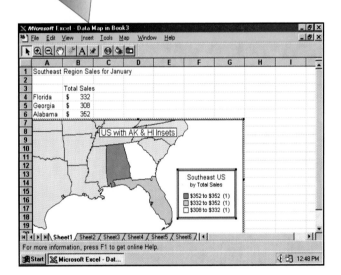

4 Now, let's enlarge the map so that the legend doesn't cover up map information. Place the mouse pointer over the middle handle in the bottom portion of the map until you see the mouse pointer shape change to a two-headed arrow. Then, drag down to row 20—as far as Excel will let you drag without repositioning the window.

5 Repeat the process on the right side of the map, dragging the middle handle out to column G. ■

WHY WORRY?

If the legend still covers part of the map, move the legend by selecting it and dragging it. Also, keep enlarging the map as needed.

Modifying Map Text

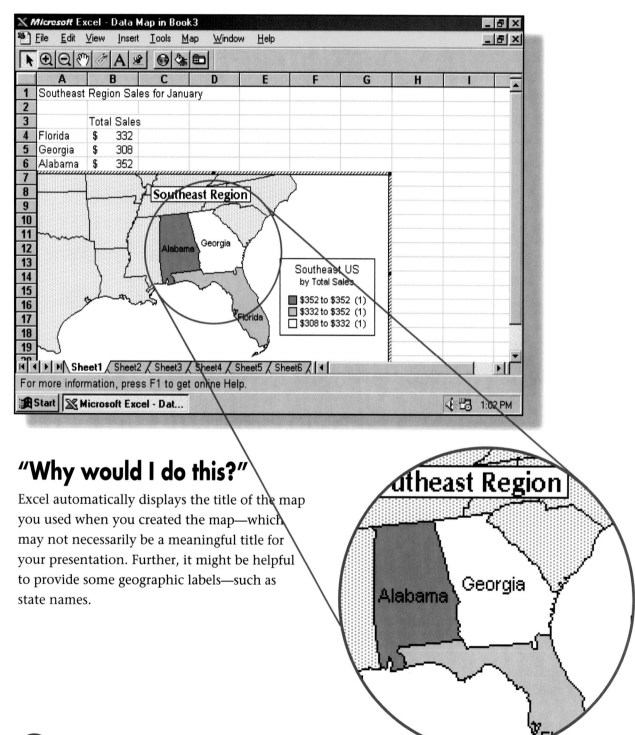

"Why would I do this?"

Excel automatically displays the title of the map you used when you created the map—which may not necessarily be a meaningful title for your presentation. Further, it might be helpful to provide some geographic labels—such as state names.

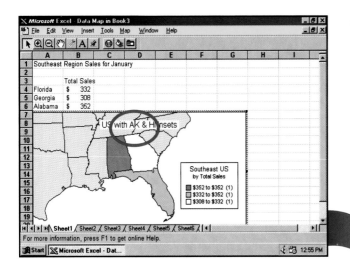

1 Double-click the title Excel provided on the map. You'll see a cross-hatched insertion point.

2 Press **Backspace** or **Delete** to remove the characters you see, and then type a new title and press **Enter**—in this case, type **Southeast Region**.

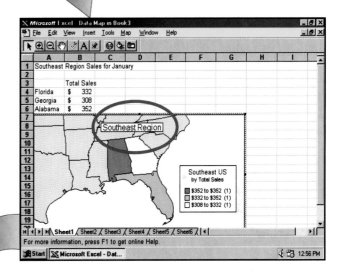

3 Click the title to select it and then click the *right* mouse button. From the shortcut menu that appears, choose **Format Font**. Excel displays the Font dialog box.

227

4 Choose a new font or add enhancements such as bold to the current font and choose **OK**. In this figure, I changed the font and added bold.

5 Now, let's label the states. Click the **Label** tool in the Map toolbar. Excel displays the Map Labels dialog box.

WHY WORRY?

When you finish labeling the map, press **Esc** to deselect the last label and click the pointer tool so that Excel won't try to add additional labels.

6 Click **OK** to accept the defaults and move the mouse pointer into the map area. As it passes over a state, you'll see the state's name. Click to place the label on the map. Repeat Steps 5 and 6 for each state you want to label. ■

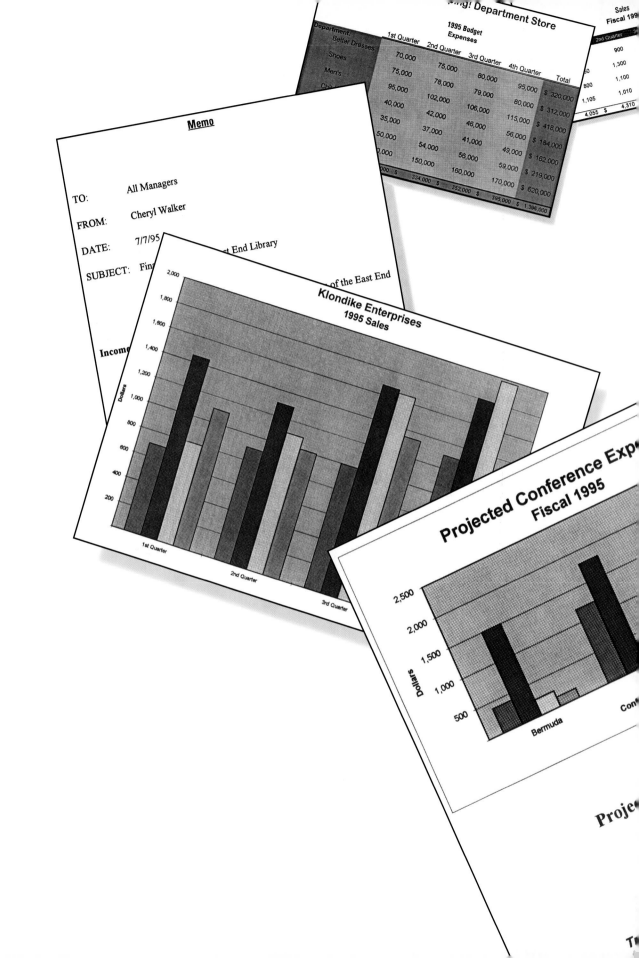

PART VIII

Document Gallery

231

Filling a Range,
p. 51

Entering Text and
Numbers, p. 36

Totaling Cells
with the SUM
Function, p. 88

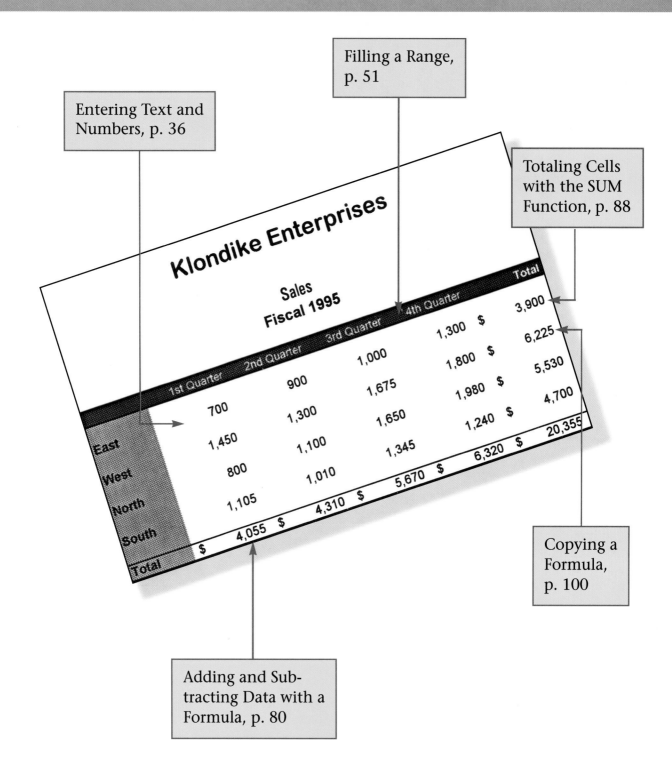

Copying a
Formula,
p. 100

Adding and Sub-
tracting Data with a
Formula, p. 80

Create a Company Sales Report

1 Type the title, column headings, row headings, and numbers. See this task for help on this step:

2 Enter a formula to add the first column of numbers. These tasks cover addition formulas:

3 Copy the formula across the total row. These tasks cover copying a formula:

4 Change the format of the entire worksheet to the **Classic 2** format. See this task:

5 Save and print the sales report. See these tasks on saving and printing:

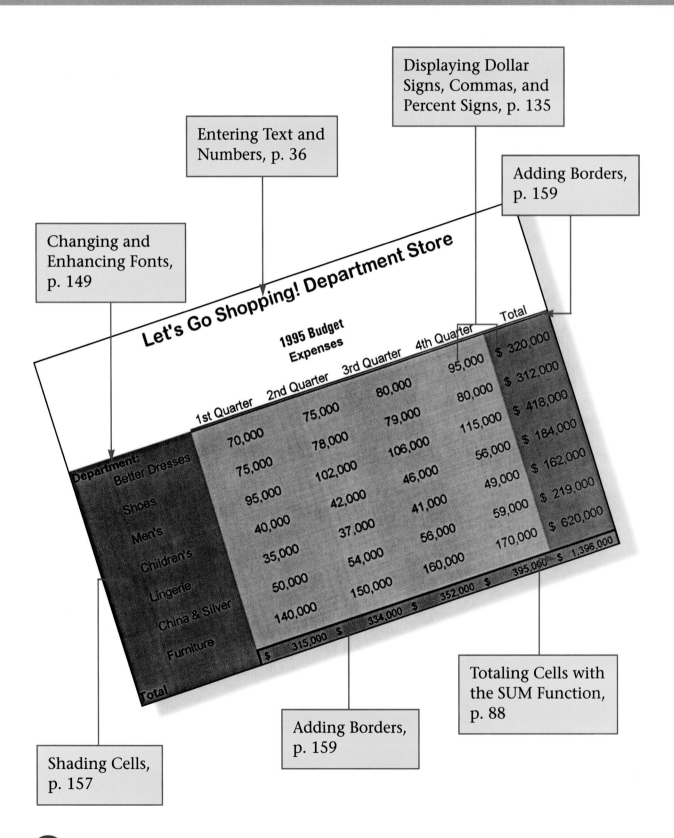

Displaying Dollar Signs, Commas, and Percent Signs, p. 135

Entering Text and Numbers, p. 36

Adding Borders, p. 159

Changing and Enhancing Fonts, p. 149

Let's Go Shopping! Department Store

1995 Budget Expenses

Department:	1st Quarter	2nd Quarter	3rd Quarter	4th Quarter	Total
Better Dresses	70,000	75,000	80,000	95,000	$ 320,000
Shoes	75,000	78,000	79,000	80,000	$ 312,000
Men's	95,000	102,000	106,000	115,000	$ 418,000
Children's	40,000	42,000	46,000	56,000	$ 184,000
Lingerie	35,000	37,000	41,000	49,000	$ 162,000
China & Silver	50,000	54,000	56,000	59,000	$ 219,000
Furniture	140,000	150,000	160,000	170,000	$ 620,000
Total	$ 315,000	$ 334,000	$ 352,000	$ 395,000	$ 1,396,000

Totaling Cells with the SUM Function, p. 88

Adding Borders, p. 159

Shading Cells, p. 157

234

Create a Departmental Budget

1 Type the information in the budget worksheet. See these tasks for help on this step:

Entering Text and Numbers   *Task 9, p. 36*

Totaling Cells with the SUM Function   *Task 25, p. 88*

Filling a Range   *Task 14, p. 51*

2 Format the numbers for each quarter with commas to zero decimal places. Format the numbers in the total row with dollar signs and zero decimal places. See these tasks:

Displaying Dollar Signs, Commas, and Percent Signs   *Task 39, p. 135*

Specifying Decimal Places   *Task 40, p. 138*

3 Format the headings by changing the fonts and font sizes and adding bold. You can find help in this task:

Changing and Enhancing Fonts   *Task 44, p. 149*

4 Insert a double underline border beneath the column headings. Also, add an outline border to the numbers in the total row. See this task:

Adding Borders   *Task 47, p. 159*

5 Add light gray shading to the numbers in each column except for the last row (total row). Then change the color of the cells in the total row and the total column to aqua. See this task:

Shading Cells   *Task 46, p. 157*

6 Save and print the budget. See these tasks on saving and printing:

Saving a Workbook   *Task 31, p. 112*

Printing the Worksheet   *Task 54, p. 179*

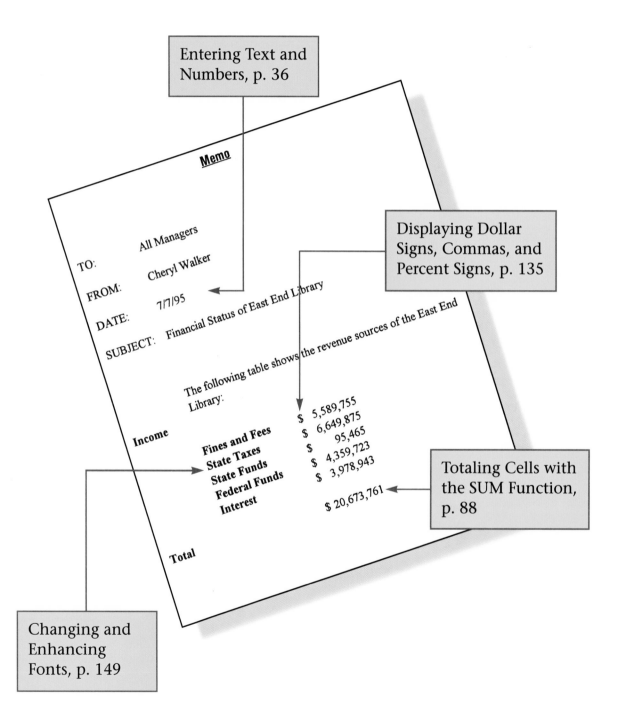

Entering Text and Numbers, p. 36

Displaying Dollar Signs, Commas, and Percent Signs, p. 135

Totaling Cells with the SUM Function, p. 88

Changing and Enhancing Fonts, p. 149

Memo

TO: All Managers

FROM: Cheryl Walker

DATE: 7/7/95

SUBJECT: Financial Status of East End Library

The following table shows the revenue sources of the East End Library:

Income

Fines and Fees	$ 5,589,755
State Taxes	$ 6,649,875
State Funds	$ 95,465
Federal Funds	$ 4,359,723
Interest	$ 3,978,943

Total $ 20,673,761

Create a Memo with a Table

1 Type the memo including the table. See this task for help on this step:

Entering Text and Numbers   *Task 9, p. 36*

2 Create a SUM formula to add the numbers. See this task:

Totaling Cells with the SUM Function   *Task 25, p. 88*

3 Format the numbers by adding a dollar sign and no decimal places. See these tasks:

Displaying Dollar Signs, Commas, and Percent Signs   *Task 39, p. 135*

Specifying Decimal Places   *Task 40, p. 138*

4 Boldface and underline the title MEMO. Then change the font for the memo headings to Times New Roman 12 point. Then boldface the memo headings. Also, boldface the headings and subheadings in the table. This task covers font changes, bold, and underline:

Changing and Enhancing Fonts   *Task 44, p. 149*

5 Save and print the memo. See these tasks on saving and printing:

Saving a Workbook   *Task 31, p. 112*

Printing the Worksheet   *Task 54, p. 179*

Formatting the Title,
p. 199

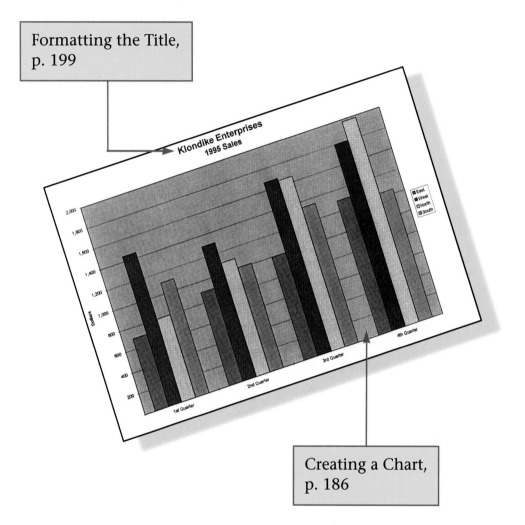

Creating a Chart,
p. 186

Create a Column Chart

1 Using the company sales report, create a column chart on a separate sheet to show quarterly sales by territory. The data you want to chart includes the column headings, row headings, and the sales figures. Do not include the totals. See these tasks for help on this step:

Selecting Cells	*Task 8, p. 30*
Creating a Chart	*Task 55, p. 186*

2 Change the font for the chart title to Times New Roman 18. Also, boldface the title. See this task for help on this step:

Formatting the Title	*Task 59, p. 199*

3 Save and print the chart. See these tasks on saving and printing:

Saving a Workbook	*Task 31, p. 112*
Printing a Chart	*Task 65, p. 215*

Creating a Chart, p. 186

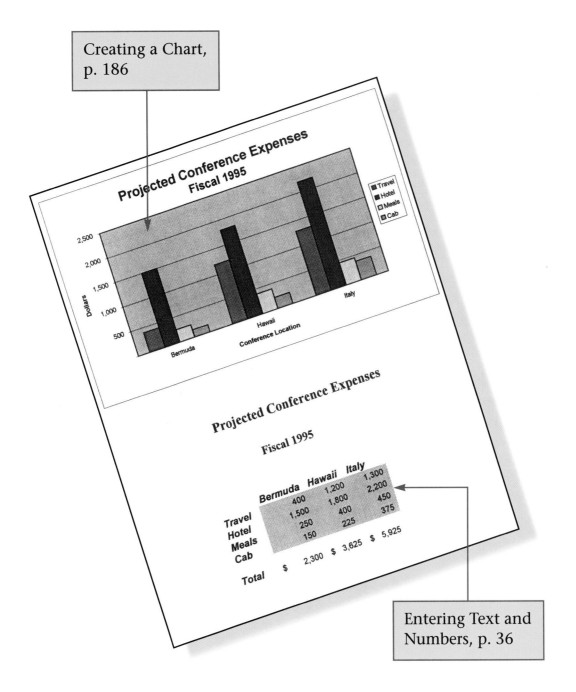

Entering Text and Numbers, p. 36

Create an Expense Report and a Column Chart

1 Type the expense report in the worksheet. See this task for help on this step:

    Entering Text and Numbers   *Task 9, p. 36*

2 Enter a formula to subtract expenses from the income. See this task:

    Adding and Subtracting Data with a Formula   *Task 23, p. 80*

3 Copy the formula across the total row. These tasks cover copying a formula:

    Filling a Range   *Task 14, p. 51*

    Copying a Formula   *Task 29, p. 100*

4 Select the data you want to chart: the column headings, row headings, and the expenses. Do not include the totals. Be sure to plot the data series in rows. See these tasks for help on this step:

    Selecting Cells   *Task 8, p. 30*

    Creating a Chart   *Task 55, p. 186*

5 Create a column chart on the worksheet. See this task:

    Creating a Chart   *Task 55, p. 186*

6 Save and print the balance sheet and the column chart. See these tasks on saving and printing:

    Saving a Workbook   *Task 31, p. 112*

    Printing a Chart   *Task 65, p. 215*

PART IX

Reference

- Quick Reference

- Toolbar Guide

Quick Reference

If you cannot remember how to access a particular feature, use this quick list to find the appropriate command. For more detailed information, see the tasks in Parts I through VII of this book.

Command Reference

Feature	Shortcut Command	Key
Alignment	Format Cells (Alignment tab)	Ctrl+1 (Alignment tab)
Border	Format Cells (Border tab)	Ctrl+1 (Border tab)
Close File	File Close	(none)
Column Delete	Edit Delete Entire Column	(none)
Column Hide	Format Column Hide	(none)
Column Insert	Insert Columns	(none)
Column Width	Format Column Width	(none)
Copy	Edit Copy	Ctrl+C
Edit Cell	(none)	F2
Exit	File Exit	Alt+F4
Font	Format Cells (Font tab)	Ctrl+1 (Font tab)
Format Numbers	Format Cells (Number tab)	Ctrl+1 (Number tab)
Go To	Edit Go To	F5 or Ctrl+G
Help	Help	F1
Move	Edit Cut, then Edit Paste	Ctrl+X, then Ctrl+V
New File	File New	Ctrl+N
Open File	File Open	Ctrl+O
Page Break	Insert Page Break	(none)

Feature	Shortcut Command	Key
Preview	File Print Preview	(none)
Print	File Print	Ctrl+P
Range Fill	Edit Fill Series	(none)
Range Name	Insert Name Define	(none)
Replace	Edit Replace	Ctrl+H
Row Delete	Edit Delete Entire Row	(none)
Row Height	Format Row Height	(none)
Row Hide	Format Row Hide	(none)
Row Insert	Insert Rows	(none)
Save	File Save	Ctrl+S
Save As	File Save As	(none)
Shade	Format Cells (Patterns tab)	Ctrl+1 (Patterns tab)
Sort Data	Data Sort	(none)
Undo	Edit Undo	Ctrl+Z

Toolbar Guide

The Standard and Formatting toolbars appear at the top of the Excel screen and contain many tools that let you accomplish Excel tasks more quickly. To use a toolbar button, simply click the button.

Standard Toolbar

Button	Name	Purpose
	New Workbook	Creates a new workbook
	Open	Opens a workbook
	Save	Saves a workbook
	Print	Prints a worksheet
	Print Preview	Previews a print job
	Spelling	Checks the spelling in a worksheet
	Cut	Cuts a range to the Clipboard
	Copy	Copies a range to the Clipboard

Button	Name	Purpose
	Paste	Pastes a range
	Format Painter	Copies formats
	Undo	Undoes the preceding action
	Repeat	Repeats the preceding action
Σ	AutoSum	Inserts a SUM formula
*f*ₓ	Function Wizard	Inserts and edits functions
	Sort Ascending	Sorts data in ascending order
	Sort Descending	Sorts data in descending order
	ChartWizard	Accesses the ChartWizard
	Map	Creates a map
	Drawing	Displays the Drawing toolbar
100%	Zoom Control	Controls the display of a worksheet
	TipWizard	Provides tips on Excel operations
	Help	Provides on-screen Help about Excel

Formatting Toolbar

Button	Name	Purpose
Arial	Font	Changes font
10	Font Size	Changes font size
B	Bold	Makes cell contents bold
I	Italic	Makes cell contents italic
U	Underline	Makes cell contents underlined
	Align Left	Aligns cell entries to the left

Button	Name	Purpose
	Center	Centers entries in a cell
	Align Right	Aligns cell entries to the right
	Center Across Columns	Centers text across columns
	Currency Style	Adds dollar signs to numbers
	Percent Style	Adds percent signs to numbers
	Comma Style	Adds commas to numbers
	Increase Decimal	Adds one decimal place to number
	Decrease Decimal	Removes one decimal place from number
	Borders	Adds a border to a selected range
	Color	Adds a color to a range
	Font Color	Adds color to a font

Index